The Magic of Soccer

The
Magic of
SOCCER

An American's Appreciation

JERRY TRECKER

Atheneum   *New York* *1982*

Library of Congress Cataloging in Publication Data

Trecker, Jerry.
The magic of soccer.

1. Soccer.   I. Title.
GV943.T68   1981   796.334′2   81–66004
ISBN 0–689–11144–4   AACR2

For my family and my mentors, men at The Hartford Courant *who helped define the craft.*

Contents

The Magic of Soccer

1.

The Magic of Soccer

Every sporting event has its own mood, keys that arrange the variety of activities into a feeling recalled long after the individual event fades from the mind. Baseball is peanuts and hot dogs, wandering vendors, and foul balls coming back into the crowd. Football, the smell of burning leaves, mums sold by enterprising fraternity brothers, the inevitable organized cheering, apparently so artificial, yet managing to entrap the audience with its own momentum so that, when the excitement mounts, you forget the leaders and the cheers have their own spontaneity. Basketball and hockey conjure sensations of heated arenas, smoke-filled corridors, the smell of cooking oil, and the lingering staleness of spilled beer on narrow passageways. They also channel the power of the closely knit crowd, a collective scream of delight or disappointment that mirrors a scoreboard, the sound of relief or desperation at the nearly scored goal.

In Britain, soccer is color, song, and passionate caring, and home of my most affecting memories.

I had seen the game only in North America, and never at the professional level except for a handful of lackluster exhibition matches by touring teams. My first impression of soccer in England was breathtaking. The afternoon was heat wave warm by London standards—people would actually collapse from the 75-degree sunshine later that day and the match at Tottenham Hotspur's White Hart Lane, a fabled football venue in North London, was special. It was opening day of the 1968 season and the opponent was none other than Arsenal, one of London's most famous teams.

Arsenal had been the first soccer team to take more form for me than those tiny lines of type in the Sunday newspaper that faithfully report "British football Results." Arsenal was always listed first when at home, the matches always listed alphabetically by division. I recall noticing those results back in preteen days when the University of Southern California football team was the only football I had ever heard of, unclear as to why the *Los Angeles Times* should publish British football results to begin with, even more uncertain why English teams never seemed to score even a single touchdown but decided all of their games in field goals and safeties, not to mention their strange ability to score one point.

My parents didn't know what British football was either, but when soccer began to have meaning, in Connecticut instead of California, they took me to an unusual bookstore in upper Manhattan. There, amidst a collection of volumes mostly imported from faraway places, was *Forward Arsenal* by Bernard Joy. Joy was to become the introduction to many things about the game, not least to the marvelous language of soccer as it had been developed by British journalists.

Details of the book are hazy now, but the cover showed an action shot of Arsenal men in the baggy shorts and heavy boots of the immediate post-World-War-II years. The dust jacket reported that journalist Joy had once been a player on some of the great Arsenal sides. Inside was his story of the team, probably not all that unlike the many "team histories" you can gather easily enough in the United Kingdom today, but that was the first team story I ever read, so it remains *Hamlet* among a collection of drama, a Memling among a display of minor masters. The names of Hapgood, Drake, and Herbert Chapman, the W-M formations and the introduction of the center back, the FA (Football Association) Cup loss to Walsall, and the great run of success in the 1930s—these all became part of my sporting memory before there was any real context for them. It was strange, some would say peculiar, to gather a fount of information about people never seen, and never likely to be seen either; but that book made sense to someone trying to discover more about the game. It led to roads unknown and scenes quite unexpected.

That was 1956, just after I had discovered that newspapers would actually pay people to do what I liked doing: go to sports events for free and then write stories about them. A combination of luck and others' lethargies had made me correspondent for our high school soccer team and this responsibility soon grew with the paper's discovery that I did not mind traveling to watch others play all other sports. Like most American kids, I knew the batting averages by heart, held my breath when Don Larsen faced Dale Mitchell in the bottom of the ninth and wondered aloud how this thing called professional football could ever match the college game for thrills and atmosphere. Soccer at this time was a minor fall diversion, my interest in it linked to the school, my real enthusiasm being saved for coverage of basketball and baseball. But even then soccer was already pushing football aside in my mind and would, in a decade, take total control.

Forward Arsenal was part of the reason for this, the book offering me the chance to become an expert in an obscure area, an attraction hard to deny. Some people gathered information about baseball, automobiles, airplanes, the Civil War, or movie stars. I began to collect data on soccer players and soccer teams. It was painstaking at first, no real source of material readily at hand, no one to ask questions of. Sadly, it required a tragedy to focus the search and define the avenues of education that would shape my soccer future.

Spring 1958 conjures terrible memories for anyone connected with soccer. Manchester United's marvelous young team was shattered (eight players, three officials, and eight newspapermen died) in the crash of a plane returning from a match in West Germany. Even though soccer was largely unknown in the United States, the disaster made front-page news, albeit briefly. United became larger than life after that, and stayed on our sports pages, by managing to fight its way to the Football Association Cup final of 1958.

It was in search of more information about them, trying to find the elusive midweek result of a replayed match or postponed League game, that I discovered the shortwave radio and the British Broadcasting Corporation. So began what has become a twenty-five-year course in soccer by radio taught by the precise, witty, observant men who man the boxes for the BBC. My Saturday morning ritual became listening to commentaries, conjuring visions of the play itself, the crowds, and the settings. There were ninety-two club names to learn, a myriad of competitions to unscramble (a European soccer team competes in its league, a national cup, and a league cup and, possibly, in one European tournament, all competitions running relatively simultaneously), and reams of players' names to associate with their teams. To a born sports nut, the challenge was too enticing to overlook and someone who knew every baseball player on sixteen major league teams could surely acquire a working knowledge of the starting lineups of Britain's major soccer squads. That led to more books, the discovery of obscure places where a London Sunday newspaper could be purchased a few days late, those precious lineups and standings to be carefully cut out and saved for further study. The information slowly began to make some sense, although I cannot recall the moment when it all had a certain meaning and stopped being a mere collection of items with no fixed point.

I have since been reminded of how complicated the soccer world really is. In those earliest days I was literally struggling with the simplest of questions (Who was in what League? What was promotion and relegation? Did a game count if it didn't last the full 90 minutes? What was the difference between the Scottish Cup and the Scottish League Cup?). Today I know that even people knowledgeable in the game can get easily confused. Beyond the United Kingdom there are something like one hundred and fifty nations that play soccer, many with their own famous teams, players, stadia, their own achievements and disappointments, an entire history to be learned. I spent a decade trying to get the U.K. firmly under control and a lifetime since with the rest of it, the challenge now including the excursion into different languages, that radio tuned to matches from all over the globe, some of the reports intelligible only to the extent that a player's name can be culled from a collection of sounds, the explosion of a crowd signaling action, and an announcer's frenzy indicating a goal. In an age of television, I was hooked on radio. The same way as those people who drive their cars to a corner of Iowa to maximize their chance of hearing a University of Kentucky basketball game, I would persist in listening when reception conditions were so poor that only the static seemed to have definition. Sitting at home on a wintry morning, I could not help but wonder if *anybody* else in North America listened to matches from Italy, Belgium, Portugal, France, and Spain, then spun the dial to acquire the results from Holland and hoped for reasonable conditions in the late afternoon so that contests from Brazil or Chile would come in loud and clear. The fact that Italian, French, Portuguese, Spanish, and Dutch were languages I could only barely understand was no factor. With perseverance, anything can be understood if you give it time and are willing to do some basic research. The number system is, of course, vital, but soccer helps in that regard since you don't really need to know any number above five. The names of the teams and the players can do pretty much the rest. At some point I became aware that I knew what was going on and what those words meant, but only after years of listening, buying newspapers in the languages, and devoting hours to the task. A crazy pursuit, perhaps, but one that brought its own reward whenever a foreign-born reader would be kind enough to register shock at the fact that I possessed no accent, was, really, born in America and did, really, get the information right in the morning paper that day.

But this was the book knowledge of the game. There remained the immersion in the actual thing itself. It seems light years ago, but soccer in the American schools was then almost a totally different game. My high school was somewhat rare in the very fact it had a team, albeit playing strange rules: There were kick-ins from the touchlines instead of the universal throw-in; games were played in quarters instead of halves; matches ended in draws but were sometimes decided by the number of corner kicks a team had obtained; and, of course, there was free substitution, designed to allow more people to play. To someone with no experience of international soccer, viewing the American scholastic version is hardly the best way to understand the world's game.

White Hart Lane in North London that 1968 Saturday afternoon was far more than those names and statistics, though I had been well prepared intellectually for the images that were to become real, had even ventured far afield in North America to sample the available products. I knew, for instance, that most spectators at a British game stood throughout to watch the play, although this was unheard of in an American stadium. I knew that most fans arrived at games by train or bus, but was quite unprepared for the fact that the stadium was tucked in a residential-industrial section and that I would almost be upon it before I could see it. I knew that British soccer teams played every Saturday, the games starting promptly at 3 P.M., but was not prepared for the fact that everybody arrived between 2:30 and 3, there being no preliminary activities to attract early comers. It meant that instead of a leisurely approach to the ticket windows there was a chaotic rush, the staid English who line up so peacefully, so respectfully, so intelligently for buses and subways, now breaking ranks and making for the entrances in phalanxes that must be subliminal reminders of Roman occupation long before Harold of Wessex ever had to worry about any Normans.

The train to Tottenham itself was the first introduction to the real game. From Liverpool Street station my wife and I took a soccer special to White Hart Lane. The carriage occupants all wore scarves of their team, that day, either the red and white of Arsenal or the blue and white of Spurs. *Forward Arsenal* had contained pictures of those fans and much was made of the team colors, so it was even easy to determine which battery of supporters we were among. The good-natured banter (in those prehooligan days) of the fans was much harder to follow. The London-accented English was not yet easily tuned by my American ear, but the rhythm of the speech, the very songlike quality in the rise and fall of intonation was recognized and the sounds heard on the shortwave radio when the fans broke into song at British matches came back to mind.

We made our way to the stadium with the aid of two British boys who appeared to be fascinated by the fact that we were American.

"My father comes from Cincinnati," one told my wife, rather as if Cincinnati were somewhere near Atlantis, the Olympian gods equally close by the Ohio River. "Ever hear of it?"

Assured that the home of the Reds was, indeed, a bastion of American life and worthy of the awe that very name seemed to inspire, the guide subtly lost a pace to inform me, the protector apparently, that "you should go right 'round to the side and ask for stand seats, because you would not want a lady on the ends. There's likely to be a punch-up or two." Good advice, followed ever since, reinforced once inside the ground by the sight of the St. John's ambulance workers carrying out the wounded just minutes before kickoff. Teenage fans follow their own rituals on a British soccer Saturday, fighting a part of it, but it was largely a well-behaved crowd of fifty thousand.

There were no seats available, so side terraces had to be the order of the afternoon, remarkably cheap at six shillings. Through the narrowest of openings we passed, each thinking of some obese friends at home who could never attend a game in England since they would be literally wedged eternally between the ticket seller and the ancient iron turnstile he operates with his foot.

A tunnel led us quickly to a shaft of light and a mass of people the likes of which I had never encountered. We forced our way into the brilliant sunlight, then struggled, pushed, escaped to the left, wondered finally if the tiniest open patch of concrete might materialize for us to stand on. There could be no question of watching a game in this mass of humanity. Indeed we could barely get around in a position facing the field of play. At last we spied some upper-level terraces that were open. Setting course for the nearest stairway we re-grouped for another climb through still another tunnel and finally to a place of our own and a view of the playing surface itself.

Green, brilliant, lush, and miraculous. Having come from a Northeastern United States summer that turned lawns to straw by mid-July and threatened to reduce the nearest baseball diamond to pure dust by September, it was an almost forgotten green. Here, too, was a soccer pitch that was entirely grass, no infield slashed across one end, no football markings to disturb the purity of the penalty area. The two halfway flags joined the corner flags in symmetry. It looked as if no soccer boot had ever trod on that turf, so pristine was the setting.

The eye swept upward to the blue painted letters on the stand opposite our terrace—THFC (Tottenham Hotspur Football Club) interlaced in a script inside a circle. Flags flew above the stadium's main stand. Sparkling white poles held the roof of that main Victorian edifice complete with cupola. All around packs of people jammed the terraces at either end, scarves held up in parallel style as they swayed back and forth, chanting "Ar-sen-al" and "Tott-en-ham," the latter delivered staccato in reply to the more litanized delivery of the visitors. The season opener was now but five minutes away and the fans were creating their own mood. It is a scene repeated across the U.K. every Saturday during the long August to May soccer season, but that first day remains as evergreen as the pitch on which the match was played.

What remained to come were the teams, the twenty-two men who would turn *Forward Arsenal* into actual experience. Arsenal was first onto the pitch, bright red jerseys and white pants above red socks. Spurs in their white tops with dark blue shorts came next, each team taking residence in half the field. Next came the officiating trio, like Coldstream Guards on the march, referee with white ball tucked firmly under an arm, linesmen moving to position. A sound of the whistle brought the two captains to the center of the pitch for the coin toss, the referee looked at his watch after checking to make sure both teams were ready to play and kickoff came exactly at 3 P.M. as advertised. There was no national anthem.

I was not at all prepared for that. Games did not begin at home without "The Star Spangled Banner," played by some Gladys Goodding at the organ or sung by some operatic personality at home plate for a World Series. Indeed, games never simply *began,* they unfolded out of some kind of ceremony. There was a matter-of-factness about the start of this soccer match in London, a crisp, let's-get-going attitude which remains symbolic today, long after I have come to accept it as simple fact. A brief loudspeaker reading of the names of the substitutes, the referee's whistle to call the captains to centerfield, the toss, and then the start: clean, without fanfare, much like starting another day at work. Soccer is so much a part of the scene, as common as breakfast, lunch, and dinner that it needs no introduction.

Unlike any match previously seen, this one took place at breathtaking speed, conjuring an image of ice hockey as the players swept up and down the pitch. The ball moved at a pace never seen before, surging first to one end, then the other, swept along by the songs of the crowd, which made the first five minutes a crescendo of noise. After all these years—after uncounted games seen at top level in many of the great stadia of Europe have brought temperance to the initial impression and reveals that the game's majesty lies not solely in speed, but in the manner in which speed is created from apparent inertia—why is it that everything seemed so fast that afternoon? Perhaps it was the overpowering of the senses with all the phenomena bombarding an impressionable mind. As likely, it was the combination of expectation meeting realization, the fact that after a decade of reading and listening to the BBC, here was a real First Division match in Britain. That would suffice were it not for the fact that there have been other occasions when the same sensation of speed and precision have intruded again: a game in Saarbrucken, between Second Division West German sides; the opening phase of the second half in Cologne when West Germany played its first 1977 international without Franz Beckenbauer, found itself lifted on a wave and destroyed Northern Ireland in 25 minutes of absolute genius; an insignificant schoolboy match in Dundee where a swirling August wind could not force the ball out of touch, so measured were many of the passes. There are, it seems, times when the game is played at super pace, times when emotion and energy propel the players, seem to transfer the intensity to everyone and even the lovely game itself.

Surely Tottenham and Arsenal produced a memorable match that August afternoon, one when the speed of play even deceived the Spurs' defense and the first goal I ever saw across the Atlantic was deflected into his own net by an unfortunate Tottenham defender. I did not leave the arena feeling he was at fault, wondering instead how defenders ever managed to get into position to make the plays, so speedy were the forwards, so intricate the weaving maneuvers to set them free, so accurate the crosses flung in from the wings, catapulted as if at some lord's castle by an army of barons bent on one more conquest for king or money.

White Hart Lane had the atmosphere that made soccer what it was and translated those words of Bernard Joy into visible action. The intensity of the crowd's involvement in the game was unlike anything at home. Certainly an American crowd cheering its collegiate heroes is involved in the business of enjoyment and winning, but the British crowd had been made up of different elements, more varied, drawing from a bigger social cross section. Of the popular American games, basketball and hockey come closest to capturing the feel of big-time soccer, the fans close enough to the action so that they can communicate directly with the players. Consider that the fans standing on the terraces in the typically compact European stadium can reach out and touch players as they retrieve a ball, note that anybody who takes a throw-in along the touchline can speak with a spectator standing right next to him, then recall that crowds of over fifty thousand can be packed into these grounds. The boundaries to the player must seem entirely human.

Is this making too much of a game? Likely, but mere games do become more than mere *parts* of a nation's culture and personal identity. Games do have the power to transport you back to the nicest moments, when all is right with life and land, producing a sense of *déjà vu* in no way disconcerting. Indeed, it may be what many of us seek when we go to the park.

At White Hart Lane in 1968 everything was new,

clean, and dramatic. But the experience did not end when the referee blew the final whistle, continuing into the streets surrounding the ground, back through the return trip into London, finally onto the front pages of the specially produced newspapers that appeared as if by magic by the time the train arrived, complete with final scores and stories of the day's play.

That was introduction to the real game, introduction with the power to capture. From that moment, the Red Sox really held no interest, work was the means by which I raised the money to spend summers in European cities with famous soccer teams. Why else would anyone visit Saint-Étienne instead of Lyon? The three-star restaurants are in Lyon, but the best team in France plays out of Saint-Étienne, some forty minutes down the rail line in the center of an industrial setting that mirrors Pittsburgh, not the Côte d'Azur.

I have visited Saarbrucken and Aachen, Strasbourg and Ostend, Falkirk and Neustad, all in pursuit of a game, watched factory teams play in Heidelberg, youth teams in North Cologne, children in a suburb of Brussels, wandered through the shops of Amsterdam, Dusseldorf, Nuremberg, Munich, and Paris, looking not for designer fashions but for team patches, pins, old programs. Itineraries for foreign travels have been dictated by the schedule produced by some soccer secretary, not by the posters or guidebooks that tout a nation's scenery.

Now that the game has come to America, transported here with an almost missionary zeal by its promoters, I find myself trapped betwen memory and expectation. To some extent, like the European fan who mirrors every modern game against a boyhood recall, I measure the sport in the United States against years of viewing it in its native setting. That makes me a purist according to some American soccer people (purist is not a word used in praise in our modern age), especially when I suggest that we have yet to enter completely the total world of the sport.

There is a magic in it worth keeping pure, an attraction that crosses national borders and languages. Searching for mere knowledge of the game, I found pleasure, which in the final analysis is what games are about.

2.

The World Game at a Glance

At the first Trans Atlantic Challenge Cup final in Giants Stadium, with 60,384 fans making a Memorial Day afternoon into a triumph for the North American Soccer League, former Vancouver President John Best, part of the NASL pretty much from the beginning, paused to reflect on what the afternoon meant: "I came here when it (the NASL) all first started and when I moved to Vancouver the thing I began talking about was that the NASL championship is only the first step. There's a whole world of high quality soccer out there and our objective has to be to get into it."

Best was a five-time All-Star in the NASL in his early career in North America, those days of the 1970s when the league was struggling for identity and survival. The ex-Liverpool man pinpointed the attraction of the sport, the major reason why so many in the United States and Canada have persevered through the hardest times. International soccer is the lure, the true difference. Although there are world championships in other areas, none can claim the kind of ongoing activity of soccer, which builds its interest around the existence of several kinds of competitions involving countries or club sides from the nations of the world. This world has ignored American soccer for so long for the simple reason that our representatives, whether club or country, have not been able to achieve results at that level. With the advent of the 1980s, that is changing.

Most dramatically, the premier competition, the World Cup, is finding space for eight more sides when the countries convene in Spain for the 1982 championship. The United States will not be among those twenty-four qualifiers for the native talent in America is not yet strong enough to overcome the very real obstacles that lie in our qualifying path. As national team coach Walt Chyzowych put it, "I think 1982 can be used as a barometer for the remaining two World Cups (in the decade) for the United States. This will be the best group of players we've ever had, and we'll see how quickly they've arrived in relation to the past. What we are searching for in the 80s is to qualify for the Olympic Games (the U. S. did in 1980, then boycotted Moscow) and a World Cup. Getting there is the final shot needed to accelerate the sport nationwide."

Certainly American qualification for a World Cup will focus more media attention on the game. Getting to Colombia in 1986 or some place to be determined, maybe right at home, in 1990, would also mark the entry into that world of competition that Best speaks of, the opportunity to measure growth and development in the most testing of competitions.

To understand just how the world regards its tournaments, it is necessary to know something of their history and genesis.

The World Cup: Begun in 1930, this quadrennial event brings together all of the nations of the soccer world for a competition that requires two years to complete, more than that to organize and stage. The initial tourney was an invitation affair, won by Uruguay, the host nation, and since that time the final stages have been shared between Europe and South America, the long-time bastions of the game. Brazil, a three-time winner and permanent holder of the initial Jules Rimet Trophy, has been the most successful country in the competition, making almost national inquests when a championship is not brought home. Italy and West Germany have been the most consistently successful European sides, proud England being the only other Old World nation to have won the top prize. Argentina joins Brazil and Uruguay as Latin American nations to have ruled the soccer sphere and will carry that honor to Spain when the 1982 World Cup starts.

What began as a small affair has blossomed into the world's largest athletic competition outside the Olympics. Two years before the actual finals, nations are divided into qualifying groups by geographic sections, engaging in playoffs that whittle down the 160-strong entry to the desired size. As the number of nations competing has grown, so has the pressure to enlarge the end stages, hence the expansion from sixteen finalists, the number since the start, to twenty-four for this coming tournament. Of those twenty-four qualifiers, six will come from "new" soccer regions, our own section of the globe (North and Central America and the Carribean), Africa, and Asia. Sixteen will be drawn from the older, more established, areas and two spots belong to the host nation and the defending champion.

The World Cup offers a unique opportunity to crown a sporting champion while at the same time letting a nation like the United States measure its own growth and potential. Where countries might not be attracted to the prospect of playing against the U.S.—the old powers have everything to lose, nothing to gain, while the new regions don't figure to be much of a financial draw—the World Cup brings all teams together if they are good enough to advance to the later stages. For America, the problem has always been Mexico, the strongest soccer nation in Central America, which has stood in the United States' qualifying path for a lifetime. As the sport grows north of the Rio Grande, however, the day could come when the U.S. represents the same kind of obstacle to the Mexicans. Chyzowych foresees such a day.

"We did well enough to almost qualify against Mexico the last time (1978) and our amateur teams have proven they (Mexico) can be beaten. We eliminated them from the 1979 Pan American Games and our team did so well that they came at us with a full professional team in the Olympic qualifying tournament," he says. "Our job now is to prove that we can hang with them on the professional level. I feel that our players will rise to the occasion." The U.S. did achieve a rare win over Mexico in 1980, but it was not enough to stay alive in the tournament.

Of course, soccer aficionados are aware of the problems that confront the U.S. in preparation for international play, but the fact remains that the average American will know next to nothing about the challenges or the prospects. That is why it remains vital for our nation to break through at the top level in an attempt to focus country-wide attention on the game, for it is the World Cup that usually creates the worldwide stars. This is attributable to television, not surprisingly.

It was 1958, the emergence of Pelé in Sweden's World Cup, that first marked the role of TV in the growth of international play, but not until 1966, when England hosted the final stages, did the event reach the global follower on his little screen. By 1970, games were scheduled in Mexico with European television in mind, hence noontime starts in the blazing heat of Guadalajara and Mexico City, and subsequently tournaments have kept an eye firmly fixed on "prime time" in the Old Continent and closed-circuit television markets in the New World. The breakthrough to home television in the United States has yet to reach a major network, but American participation in Colombia could be the catalyst to such an achievement and recognition by the general public.

The World Cup will likely remain dominated by the old line powers through this century, but the movement to open its doors to teams from less powerful sections of the globe must augur well for the growth of the game. Even more so is the World Cup's stepchild, worthy of some note.

The World Youth Cup: Begun only in 1977, with major corporate sponsorship (it *is* called the Coca-Cola Youth World Cup, in fact), this tournament is the vehicle for emerging nations, although newcomers haven't won the main prize yet. Russia was the first champion and Argentina followed its World Cup success with victory at this level in 1979, but the biennial tournament affords far more opportunity for rising nations to enter the soccer limelight. The United States is a particularly apt example of a nation taking advantage of this tournament to try to build both interest and experience for playing at the higher levels.

We participated in the 1977 qualifying stages as one of the outsiders, but we came close to grabbing a place among the final sixteen for that first tourney, held in Tunisia. Third place in that Concacaf tournament (the acronym for Central and North American playing nations) was considered a major success for then unknown Americans, giving rise to hopes, perhaps premature. A temporary letdown came in 1979 when we expected to better that achievement in Honduras, but could not. But American soccer development was proven in the 1980 qualifying tournament for the 1981 World Youth finals to be played in Australia. We join Mexico as a Concacaf representative, our achievement clear.

For the first time, the United States Soccer Federation was host for a major international tournament, one that could be a trial run for a World Youth Cup itself, or maybe even a World Cup. It would have been unthinkable even a decade ago that the United States would host a qualifying of this magnitude. Yet so quick has been American progress, so dramatic the talent development, so rapid the American public's support, that 19 national youth teams spent August 1980 in Los Angeles, Dallas, Edwardsville, Illinois and Princeton, New Jersey, to fight for those two places in Australia in 1981.

Still a very young affair, the World Youth Cup did not

immediately draw entries from all of the major world soccer powers, but one suspects that it will before much longer. It has a dual advantage as testing ground for future international players (Europe has long staged yearly junior championships for national teams) and development program for emerging nations, exactly what FIFA (Federation International des Football Associations) President João Havelange of Brazil had hoped for when he proposed the event back in 1974. With a concomitant growth of "age group" tourneys around the world, this world championship is lighthouse to an expanding band of explorers.

Olympic Games: If there is a direct path for the American national team to make an impact in world soccer it is the 1984 Olympic Games, although one wonders just what the state of Olympic affairs will be by that time. The United States is to host these Games in Los Angeles, which means we shall be automatic entrants in every sport. We qualified in 1972, but that was something of a competitive disaster, and, of course, were nonstarters in 1980. It would have been valuable to measure U. S. growth had we competed in Moscow, drawn as we were with the host nation in the preliminary group, but 1984 affords a chance for the soccer players to gain the same kind of prominence as their 1980 ice hockey counterparts did at Lake Placid. There is no doubt that home field and home crowds make a difference in all sports, so prospects must be good for some kind of success in the 1984 games.

The Olympics are the least important of the major international soccer tourneys for national teams, torn as they are by the question of what constitutes an amateur. Where countries like the U.S. send relatively inexperienced teams, the East European and Asian Communist entries contain their best athletes, as evidenced by their domination of the tournament since 1956. The result has been to unbalance the tourney to such an extent that major Western European powers simply stay home and concentrate on events sponsored by FIFA and UEFA (European Football Union). Still, keeping in mind what national television exposure can do, the Americans will be looking to use this 1984 forum to advance their own soccer cause, even if success is of less international significance than standout performance in the World Cup or World Youth Cup. Should the U.S. reach a semifinal game, for instance, and the live TV cameras carry the team's effort, you cannot really predict the impact it might have on the sport.

Those three international tournaments are for national teams, sides composed of the best available players from a country. Eligibility to participate is determined by one's place of birth or residence, though there are some catches in the regulations. Some players compete for their father's homeland or mother's homeland, but no one can play for more than one nation.

Unlike national team competitions, the other world of international play is for clubs and here, especially through the New York Cosmos, the United States has already made a mark. Briefly, let's review the kinds of club tournaments available and sort out some of their history.

European Cup: The oldest of three continental tournaments, this began in 1955 and involves the league champion in each of the thirty-three UEFA member nations. It is a straight knockout competition leading to a final game in May each year, one of the big events on the European soccer calendar. Dominated in the early years by Spain's Real Madrid (they won the first five tourneys), the European Cup has highlighted a group of legendary teams: Real, Benfica of Lisbon, Ajax Amsterdam, Bayern Munich, Liverpool, and Nottingham Forest, all sides which ruled Europe.

The competition is set in motion by a draw each July, UEFA seeding the more powerful sides so they don't eliminate each other at the first hurdle. The initial round is staged in September, the second completed by November, quarterfinals come in March, and semifinals are played in April. Each contest is played over two legs, one game at each club's home with total goals determining the victor. In cases of drawn matches, UEFA uses a surprisingly effective tie-breaker method: Goals scored away from home count double. If that doesn't resolve the issue, the teams take penalty kicks after extra time in the second match.

One particularly good feature of the tourney (all three European affairs are run this way, in fact) is that there is no long-range draw established as in a tennis or basketball tournament. Instead, the survivors of each round go back into the hat and are simply paired off again. Thus, the seeding that protected the big boys at the first time is not followed thereafter and the prospects of major European clubs meeting head-on is enhanced.

Of course, North American teams aren't eligible for this tourney, or any of the European events.

European Cup Winners Cup: Patterned after the European Cup, but a younger tourney, this event is organized exactly like its parent, involving the teams that won their country's Cup competitions. In all European leagues, contrary to North American play, there are simultaneous competitions: the league action, involving a full schedule of matches on a weekly basis, and the knockout Cup tournament, which mixes together clubs from all divisions in a pure tournament setting. It is the survivors of the latter who make up the field for the Cup Winners Cup.

Cup soccer is a British invention, the venerable Football Association Cup the pattern for all of these knockout affairs. Because it allows a Third or Fourth Division team a moment of glory against a First Division side, there is a romance to that competition that is its very lifeblood. Of course, the same kind of upsets can happen in Europe, a team from Luxembourg or Iceland, for example, holding a powerhouse side from Spain or England to a draw. It rarely happens, but the chance exists and is the lure.

That can be a weakness in that some of the smaller nations tend to be dominated by a single club, which wins both league and cup in the same season. In that case, the cup runner-up gets the bid for this tournament, and that is not always a plus for the competition. The cups are noted for upsets, though, with a weak team catching a hot streak that sweeps all before it. Such may lead to success at home but rarely in the tougher arena of Europe.

UEFA Cup: Arguably this is the toughest of all three tournaments because it brings together the runners-up in regular season league action. Larger than the fields of the other, the sixty-four-team UEFA competition includes an extra round (played in late November–early December) and is usually loaded with powerful, emerging sides. As is the case in many sports, the league champion of last year may not be the best team this year, but the clubs immediately below the champion could be building toward eventual success. They're all in this tournament, which is grindingly difficult to win. Also, this is the only European meet with a two-legged final.

Copa Libertadores: South America's version of the European Cup, involving the top teams from the ten member nations of the South American Federation: Argentina, Bolivia, Brazil, Chile, Colombia, Ecuador, Paraguay, Peru, Uruguay, and Venezuela.

This tournament takes two teams from each nation and divides them into preliminary groups of four each, producing five survivors who join the Cupholder for semifinal play. Again grouped, this time in two sections of three apiece, they contest this round and the winners meet in a best-of-three series to determine the new cup winner.

Once dominated by teams from Argentina, the Copa Libertadores has opened up a bit of recent reasons to reflect the growth of soccer power in other South American nations. Colombia has produced a recent finalist while Olimpia of Paraguay broke the Argentina-Brazil hegemony by lifting the trophy in 1979.

Intercontinental Cup: Supposedly the meeting between European Cup and Copa Libertadores winner, the event has been beset by difficulties on and off the field. Marred by player and fan disputes in the 60s, the tournament lost much of its glamour in the 70s for the simple fact that Europe's champion rarely found room in its schedule to play the South American titlist. This left the European runner-up to pick up the chore, consequently devaluing the final.

Paradoxically, this once-nearly moribund affair is the best line of entry for North American teams to try and get involved in a real test of club strength. Were it possible to bring together the Cup winners and champions of Africa (they, too, stage a club championship) and Asia (they don't) with the NASL titlist at a single site for a condensed period of time, a finals of truly intriguing proportion could conceivably take place. This could be something along the lines of that Trans Atlantic Challenge Cup that the NASL got going in 1980, perhaps a blueprint type tournament for such a future interclub challenge. Getting European and South American participation would be the key.

Tour Matches: Traditionally this is the way clubs have tested themselves against another nation's sides and, not to be forgotten, picked up some cash along the way. In North America, the Cosmos are the leading touring side, composed as they are of a multinational group of players whose reputations preceded them to the Big Apple. Cosmos have done the NASL a power of public relations good by their ability to score important victories away from home, while the huge crowds which turn out to see visiting foreign sides at Giants Stadium testify to the viability of American soccer.

Malcolm Allison, the Manchester City team manager, said at that first TACC, "The great support this tournament got this time will encourage top European sides to come here and play. The atmosphere was tremendous. They really enjoy the game here." The advantage, of course, to a tournament, even of contrived value, is that it changes the contest from mere exhibition to something with a modicum of meaning. That has often been the bane of touring sides. Often they met local teams of much lesser strength, hence wound up not having to work very hard, with no need to showcase their talents under any kind of pressure. At least the existence of strong NASL teams, all of whom recognize that their reputations are vulnerable to any visiting team, can provide the kind of stiffer test that fans appreciate.

Still, there is the very inferiority complex inherent in that last statement. Touring teams often represent the "better" quality, taking it on show to the "lesser" soccer nations. That's why the burgeoning international tourneys, like these club Cup competitions have done so much to spark real interest in the game.

But where is the American role in international club play? NASL Commissioner Phil Woosnam is firm in his belief that the United States sporting public is enough different from Europe's so that any kind of international affairs have to be structured with this in mind. "International play is another dimension to the sport," he says, "but I don't think that the American people want something long and drawn-out. They need something you can get over in two weeks, where the champion will be known." It is not that fans here are unable to follow something like the elongated European tournaments with their stops and starts, simply that the sporting pattern on our side of the Atlantic is geared to the playoff or World Series type of contained championship finals. Woosnam has been moderately successful in directing the NASL's growth, even if there are those who consider his devotion to the National Football League model to be outdated, thus this transatlantic venture may eventually turn into the kind of international affair that will succeed. The first tourney, even though it suffered the bad luck of losing a big name team (Arsenal) on the eve of the affair, was extremely successful, boding well for an expanded format in the years ahead.

"When the League Cup was first introduced in England it took quite a time to build where it is now," Vancouver's Best recalled. "The response to this tournament (TACC) in Vancouver was really tremendous." Dennis Tueart, who played a couple of seasons in New York, then returned to Manchester City, acknowledged that the fans back in England might not have taken the event all that seriously when City went on tour, but noted, "I think they will do so when news gets back about the support of the fans here."

If it keeps coming back to the fans and their obvious interest in international play, that is what Best was describing initially, noting that a league championship is only the start these days. It is partly the age of television and of easy travel which makes it possible, but more the fact that soccer benefits from its world face and its collection of differing styles and tactics, items that breed endless argument as well as provide a multiplicity of points of comparison. North American soccer is on the way to proving that the blending of players from different continents and backgrounds can be achieved with more success than the critics suspected, while international tournaments have served to spread ideas in the game, most notably the transfer of coaches from nation to nation as the top clubs seek to perpetuate their own success.

If the United States' entry into the international scene has been sputtering on the back burner for decades, it has now accelerated into something meaningful with the dawn of the 80s. The immediate aims are twofold: to achieve some kind of success in a recognized national team tournament and to build a strong club relationship that will enable our professional sides to measure their growth against the best sides of the world. Each development can lead toward an extension of the game at home and to the recognition of the American player.

3.

Reporting the World Game

If you want to know what ultimately is good or bad about a sport, how to play the game, what is correct about it, why it is revered or despised, pay attention to the way it is reported across the globe. A sport has a vocabulary that is the outgrowth of a lifetime's observation. It sets the limits on achievement and provides the yardstick for recognizing greatness, applauding genius. When a vocabulary is lacking, as in the case of American soccer today, it must be borrowed and the borrowing of information about the game will play just as vitally on its growth as the manner by which our coaches and players ultimately define their roles.

Traditional soccer reporting is not so much the mere detailing of the event as review of the performance, not a retelling of instances as a weaving of tapestry whose colors highlight that which the viewing public has come to accept as the standard of play. If the Brazilian commentator shouts "G O A L L L" for what seems like 45 seconds of controlled agony and the Frenchman produces that marvelous "Ooh . . . la . . . la . . . ." at a magic moment, the same events in Britain might receive only a single word, "Brilliant," or "Rubbish." The same game, viewed through the eyes of a Brazilian might have been perfectly paced, filled with the histrionics and individual achievement that the South Americans appear to like. A European watching the same contest might complain about lack of speed or missing "vigor," detailing instead the number of times players went down with apparently "dramatic" injuries. It does, really, depend on what you expect, how you set out to define the action.

Clearly, press boxes and reporters are not universally the same. One difference between the Old World and the New is simple to define: Over there, reporters are politely, if unenthusiastically accepted; here, reporters are catered to, the greater the enthusiasm, the greater the likelihood that the host team faces a hard sell in its own town. Covering soccer starts with the writer or broadcaster's definition of task. Where the game has been part of the fabric of life since anybody can recall, the writer has a clearly defined role. He may be a reviewer, critic, spokesman for the fan. No matter how many times you travel overseas, you never quite get over the impression made by the popular press, where Monday morning's stories aren't so much details of the Saturday game, but personal narratives that resemble the words of any fan, narratives likely already said at some bar the evening of the game. The personal touch is what sells.

That most noticeable contrast between foreign soccer reporting and the kind of sports writing that appears regularly in the American press stems from the highly competitive system of journalism, particularly in Britain, and partly from the very different role played by radio and television. Unlike the United States, where most teams have broadcasting contracts, which mean that every game may be carried in some format, European soccer teams have jealously guarded their product exposure. Television coverage is limited, Brazil an exception, and radio, too, often tightly controlled by a single "match of the day" format. In some countries, notably France, Spain, and Italy, reports are carried from all First Division league games, but no game is broadcast from start to finish. This pattern will be broken for international games or a Cup final, but the writers have adapted their styles to a situation markedly different from that facing the American. Where the U.S. writer is expected to dig behind the scenes on the assumption that most interested readers have already seen, or at least heard, the match, the overseas journalist is often content to report the action of the game, leading to some stories of considerable analytic length, but containing not a single quote from a player or manager. To American readers, satiated with "I felt good" opinions from performers whose vocabulary is sometimes less developed than their sporting skills, such reporting may be a welcome respite, but it certainly presents an altered picture of the role of journalist.

Overseas, the game itself is the centerpiece and the writer is a chronicler, his often hand-written prose telephoned back to the waiting desk man as the game is played. These stories are usually descriptions of the high points, a reference to a missed chance here, a bad foul there, some tactical comments along the way. The "play by play" will usually carry through about 75 minutes, then the writer "tops" the story with a couple of paragraphs right at the end of the match. Deadlines play a part in this coverage style, but even the writers who have a full day in between game and paper's appearance don't stray very far from the pattern. In American reporting, the emphasis is on finding out what the performers thought was important, the writing style of the 70s having shifted radically from accounts of the previous decades. Now editors and, presumably, the public want stories chock full of those quotes. Indeed, "game" stories almost no longer exist.

This difference in style contributes to one of the most striking variations between America and Europe, the manner in which the press is received. United States teams all have press representatives, public relations men who smooth the path for the reporter seeking those postgame nuggets, arranging the entry into the locker room, identifying players for reporters who don't know everyone by sight, providing media guides, press notes for every match, answering the inevitable barrage of questions. While there is an adequate pregame program available at European matches, the press boxes I've been in look and feel strangely spartan to a visitor, whether at fabled Wembley or the wet-paint newness of Cologne's Mungersdorf Stadium. European writers don't expect, don't get the kind of treatment that their American counterparts deem normal.

I suspect it won't happen overseas, either, for the simplest of reasons: Reporters I've talked with would hardly stand still for a PR man explaining the game to them. They already know what their task is, what the history of the club is, who the key players are. They also don't seem to want to talk with players, preferring to let the story succeed or fail on their own insights and ideas. Even the magazinelike publications (*France Football,* an excellent weekly example) depend largely on their own writers to generate talking points, with the kinds of personality profiles that characterize a U.S. magazine largely missing. Indeed, a partial review of the soccer world's voice is illuminating.

Most accessible, naturally, is the British press because of the English language. Hence, one's first impression of soccer writing could have come from that vastly literate material produced by Geoffrey Green of the venerable London *Times,* a man who mixed soccer reports with historical and literary references of the highest quality. Not all British writers strike the educated phraseology of Green, but there is a noticeable striving for the descriptive in the English reporter's work. I'm told it was Green who once referred to a player's late-night habits as "having cut the candle in half and burning it at all four ends." Another English writer achieved just the right touch in his 1974 World Cup final report by noting that Johan Cruyff's function that fateful afternoon could be likened to a "lighthouse curiously constructed inland." The *Times,* of course, is a national newspaper in the United Kingdom, one that ranks with the *Guardian,* two newspapers that do not regard themselves as "popular." The popular journals might be (usually are) more strident in their prose, more given to the sensational headline about a relatively trivial event; yet they, too offer a major contribution to the expectations of the public by refusing to accept substandard fare.

The language of the game has evolved from this combined effort and, thankfully, British writers are as candid as literate, buoyed by their flair for understatement. As a result, we have seen some new words come into regular American soccer usage: "marking" for the defensive task of playing man-to-man; "aggro" for the little incidents which bring tempers to the surface; "touchline" for the sidelines; "byeline" for the endlines; "the box" for the penalty area. Perfectly good words already existed in American English to describe the same things; yet the influence of the British is so profound in the sport that we would hardly benefit from changing their terminology.

The British, too, have a clear idea of what they think is a well-played game, what constitutes an exciting performance. What the public wants is goal mouth action, not packed defenses and midfield surrender, which characterizes some European league play. You can be certain that on the eve of international matches, the British public will be reminded that the opposition may have a greater store of skills (sometimes true) but that this can be negated by the British ability to get "stuck in." I once had a British broadcaster tell me that West German soccer might be pretty to watch occasionally, but that the English public would never stand for such lack of action, this at a time when Beckenbauer and Company were weaving those patterns that delighted the world and, incidentally, won a World Cup. But the Englishman was right. The British public wouldn't like a steady diet of slow build-up, sixteen or seventeen passes and a shot ultimately developing, especially since their media would remind them that this wasn't the British way.

The question is, "Do writers and broadcasters reflect taste or create it?" Continual published praise of players who are quick into the tackle, midfielders who shoot as soon as they can see the other team's posts, must produce players who play this way, just as lukewarm treatment of another style will dampen enthusiasm to attempt it. The British attitude toward the Mediterranean style, for example, can be divined by almost anyone who follows the sport, the word "cynical" so often attached to the defensive attitude that prevails in a country like Italy. It may, indeed, be negative, but regularly attaching a modifier doesn't automatically make the opposed style "open" or positive. After all, there are plenty of American football coaches who might well argue that victory starts with sound defense and attack derives from it. Yet games that are defensively oriented seem automatically to be disliked by the British no matter what the outcome.

More important are the many attitudes the British have contributed, also easily recognized in the reporting of it: the appeal to objective judgment, regularly applied to teams, individuals, and referees; the expectation of standards of fair play and the rejection of the idea of "getting what you can" within the limits of the rules; the appreciation of body contact, the physical tests; the importance of team over individual. British reporters are notoriously critical of their own players so you quickly recognize that this is not a nation of yes men. Indeed, the interloper who chances upon the British soccer press, with its buckshot approach to hooliganism, fouls on the field, players being cautioned and sent off, games lacking in skill or drama, might well think the sport on its last legs. In fact, the opposite seems to be true, the public clamoring for more information, more television, more "big" games.

The objective approach to match reporting, which

may yield a story that does not flatter the home side or winds up being a chronicle of advice for the losers can make the writers less than popular figures. If the writers aren't plain "fans," most seem just as opinionated. Such reporting would not get very far in the American media, where the writer is supposed to be detached and his analysis somewhat clinical; but the lack of "passion" that characterizes our reporting is quite noticeable beside that which regularly appears in Great Britain.

The expectation of fair play, rejection of the "professional foul," time wasting, tactical closing up of the game, and some other features of modern defensive soccer are all fair game for attack in the press. Despite the wide variety of journals available, the writers are remarkably consistent in what they define as the ethics of the sport and they perform a vital function with that unity.

There is also a delightful amount of pure nationalism in soccer writing in Britain, to the extent that the Scots reporters are quick to point out flaws in the English game even as the Scots players head South after the big money and fame on that side of the River Tweed. It's not always in good fun. One column referred to Scottish fans as "drunks and psychopaths," and the hard-hitting British playing style is often seen as "intimidating" by Continental opposition. Discussions of who has the best brand of European league soccer seem never ending. The British are particularly harsh on South American players, for some reason, while sharpening their pencils to make certain everyone knows the limits of North America, too. But all the nationalism inherent in soccer reporting is no more than a reflection of nationalism on the field, now that the game has developed its face to such an extent that major competitions among countries are always under way. The press, naturally, often portrays its own heroes in the best possible light.

Since much of the game revolves around judgments made spontaneously by players, referees, and coaches, it should not come as any surprise that opinion also plays a major role in the lexicon of the game. The soccer reporter who isn't willing to put his two cents into the mixture at the end of 90 minutes apparently isn't going to get much accomplished. He must win the acceptance of players and fans, while at the same time maintaining the ability to report fairly and accurately on the event, a tightrope that must be walked, keeping the freedom to call a bad match a bad match without losing the diehard reader who never really thinks his local heroes make mistakes. Reporters in Britain, more than in the United States, make direct value judgments in the course of their reports, and their penchant for first-person accounts merely emphasizes the nature of their task.

In contrast to Britain, where the sport manages to carve out a place in just about every cranny, consider France, not only because the French have a unique kind of sporting press, but also because the fans don't exactly beat down the gates to get into matches all across the land. French daily newspapers give all sports very limited coverage, but what sets the country apart is the existence of a pure sporting press, headed by the prestigious daily *L'Équipe,* which treats soccer as page one news all the time and can wax lyrical about anything in the sport. It's a paradox that in a country that has never won a major world honor or grabbed a European Cup, there can be so many outstanding journalists and respected judges of talent. Not only were the French able to foresee the greatness of Cruyff and the potential of Holland before hardly anyone else, they have also given us the incomparable phrase that serves the modern game so well: *l'anti-jeu* (literally, nongame) for the boring, defensive tactics of so many teams. It's a term every reporter should have at his command, particularly when watching eleven men spend most of the game in their own penalty area.

The French, in fact, are contributing more to the game than just their fascination with language. They have produced some of the most interesting statistical looks at major contests, publishing shooting charts and a breakdown of attacks that may help to make the game more readily understandable, though soccer is not a sport which lends itself to numbers. Perhaps because of the international outlook of Paris, French soccer reporters also possess an eye far less provincial than some others. They concentrate more on an international view of the sport, and numerous journals carry excellent foreign reports. This would be akin to finding excellent coverage of Latin American baseball in the magazines of the U.S., although there is even less excuse for comprehensive data on Brazil appearing in Paris than there is for Caribbean baseball being followed in New York. After all, about 20 percent of baseball's major leaguers *are* Latins.

The French are highly analytical, too, attempting to pick out trends that will characterize the game before they become obvious to everyone. *France Football,* a sister publication of *L'Équipe,* is an example of this style, often devoting full pages to articles on leading players, coaches, or points of discussion in the sport. While the emphasis is on French items, to be sure, one is as likely to find the game in North America profiled at some point. Italy, too, has a collection of sporting papers and at least one journal (*Guerin Sportivo*) that rivals American fascination for statistics and French willingness to range far beyond national boundaries for stories and pictures. Italian soccer revolves around the fierce competition in its own First Division (*Serie A*) and the sometimes spectacularly variable performance of the national team, the Azzurri, whose efforts arouse a love-hate relationship that manages to span the Atlantic Ocean. Remember, this is the country that pelted its national team with eggs when it returned from World Cup '66; but it is also a land equally prepared to receive sporting giants as national heroes. In passion, the Italian)ress sometimes apparently manages to equal its fans. One of the most attractive features of *Guerin Sportivo*, in addition to its complete coverage of the Italian sporting scene, is its regular European soccer features. Like the French publications, here is a magazine that does first-class player and team profiles, especially of the teams that play prominent roles in European tournaments each year.

Everything about Italy's pressure might be said double for Brazil, at least if media intensity means anything. In Italy, the state radio covers Sunday's league games live, followed by tape-delayed TV coverage. In Brazil, which has no state-controlled pattern of broadcasting of soccer, the situation is more like the U.S. with a dramatic difference: where each U.S. major league team has its own play-by-play outlet, a Brazilian team of great stature (Rio's Flamengo, for instance) might have each game it plays carried by two or three radio stations and shown on delayed television, too. And, when a Brazilian radio station covers a game, it covers it: the ultimate in dramatic, overindulgent attention to a sporting event. Even the veterans of the North American League press office had to admit that Brazilian treatment of the 1976 Bicentennial Cup games in the U.S. exceeded anything they had seen. Watching sideline reporters, equipped with their antenna-transmitters and headphones, swing into action to interview just about anything moving on the field amazed the uninitiated. A Brazilian player is subject to this barrage of radio coverage: a play-by-play team that sometimes has two announcers who manage somehow to alternate commentary without clogging each other's air; at least one analyst; another specialist who reviews the work of the referee; and at least one reporter on the sidelines to interview substitutes, coaches, officials, players sent off, whatever comes past. No report of a game is complete until interviews from the locker room are broadcast and it may be more than an hour after the match before the station has reviewed the game, replayed the goals, interviewed several people, discussed the implications for the future, and then signed off. If this isn't broadcast overkill, it comes close, but this is Brazil we're talking about, where soccer and Carneval are tied for first place in the national interest.

All this soccer reporting is accessible to the American who wants to bother with a shortwave radio and who has a little language facility. The amount of the sport on the international air lanes is prodigious, the number of available publications in the major languages just as staggering. Even the British Broadcasting Corporation (which interrupted the transmission of extra time during England's most famous victory, the 1966 World Cup final, in order to carry a regularly scheduled newscast)

now changes its program schedule in order to accommo-
date major matches like the FA Cup or European Cup
final. The BBC also schedules three hours of sport most
every Saturday on its World Service, English and Scottish soccer the staples for about eight months of that
span. It goes without saying that many other international broadcasting services see soccer every bit as important to their schedules.

Some broadcasters have huge colonies of "overseas"
nationals to keep happy and soccer seems to be something they crave. Hence, you'll find that Radio France
International never misses the second half roundup coverage of First Division games, Radio Diffusion Portugal
is on the air every weekend with complete Division One
coverage, Radio Spain airs flash reports for all First and
Second Division contests Sunday morning, Arabic language stations relay games every weekend, and the list
goes on endlessly. Games involving World Cup qualifying or European tournaments are regularly aired by
the international services, too, so the soccer fan who
wants his coverage "live," albeit often in a language
other than English, has no shortage. He can spend North
American mornings and afternoons listening to the Old
Continent, then nights tune in on Central and South
America.

But these are all media responding to a public demand for coverage, not trying to figure out how to deal
with a rising sport. The American press faces that task,
having to adapt its soccer coverage to the style of sports
reporting that is accepted in the States, chock full of
"newsy" opinions from participants, more and more
straying away from cataloging a sequence of events.
There can be little doubt that the rest of the world sees

American flirtation with soccer a bizarre and, even, threatening event. While noting that the NASL marketing techniques have succeeded in making the game appealing to family groups and wondering how they might do the same, overseas reaction to the U.S. pro circuit has still tended to place emphasis on the fact that the level of play isn't all that it might be. One tends to think there is a bit of ethnocentricity in such carping, but there is a clear message for the Americans in the steely eye being cast from abroad. Most of the world is happy with its game and the standards it has set. It is wary of U.S. innovation and a task of the American soccer press must be to watchdog the sport with the same kind of critical, reviewer's eye that has been traditionally European. If you allow the argument that only soccer purists, many of whom happen to be writers and others close to the game, have managed to keep the sport from being "modified" for television purposes in America, then you have at least one reason to thank the traditional media for staying in its correct role. You have to doubt that the soccer public would have noticed television time outs, for instance, since this is largely the same public that doesn't really complain about the fact that American scholastic and college soccer has already been tampered with to a large extent. What the fans don't know they don't complain about, so it shall remain the task of the U.S. soccer media to be carping for a while. Without that critical reminder, there is no logical reason to think that the clubs will be prodded into improving the product as long as the fans come to see the matches.

Yet American soccer writers often face a quite considerable disadvantage in comparison to their compatriots from overseas. Few are former professional players and several may have been introduced to the game about the same time the local pro team came to town. One NASL public relations man admits, "Lots of times the guy who gets the soccer beat doesn't regard it as a reward, but after he has it for a while that usually changes. We've found our players to be very cooperative with the writers. I think they enjoy the interviews and the fuss." Still, it must be clear that it is hard to be judgmental, in the Continental sense, about a game that is still largely unfamiliar, in a setting where history and precedent make it difficult to rate the product, even if you are well versed in the game. Some of the game's critics, for instance, are the products of European childhoods and they can be accused of being overzealous sometimes in their treatment of the NASL and other soccer ventures in the United States. No, the game isn't ever going to be exactly as they recalled it.

Writers, though, may be guilty of overestimating their own importance. After twenty-five years in the business, I suppose I should cease to be surprised at the fact that many people I work with daily either don't know that I cover sports events or manage to get confused over just what newspaper I do it for. It really should come as no surprise that the print media are less important now than in the days when soccer went big time in Europe, so it is likely that America's soccer reporting will be influenced more by television and radio than by what journalists have to say. In that case, the United States is just starting to get the sport shown to them. From the middle 1970s, when it was still rare to see any soccer on the home TV set, the amount of time and space devoted to the game have increased radically. Much of the soccer is still "imported," whether it was the West German-European games that the German Educational Network packaged or the English games that received weekly airing in much of the country. The development of cable systems by the turn of the decade meant that collegiate soccer was getting real attention for the first time via ESPN, the Entertainment and Sports Programming Network, while the NASL got a boost when it signed on with two cable networks, USA and ESPN. Indoor soccer, both NASL and Major Indoor Soccer League (MISL) variety, was regularly on the cable, too, while the highly effective "road game" television policy pioneered by the National Football League was being used by the NASL in major markets like New York, where all Cosmos games away from Giants Stadium, were televised into the city.

There was national television of selected NASL games, too, although even the American Broadcasting Company, with its high interest in sports programming, was quite limited in comparison to its other major sports coverage. There is a problem that comes with increased television, however: The edited, 60-minute version of the game that comes from Germany or Britain edits out some of the sport's dull moments. Hence, when an American audience sees an unedited 90-minute game, it may be struck by an apparent slowness to the action that is not all directly related to a lower level of skills. And there is also the manner of presentation, so varied that it was still difficult to pin down an American style. The most caustic critic, a woman used to listening to shortwave radio broadcasts of games, called an NASL radio treatment "so poor that I didn't even realize it was a soccer game," referring to an announcer whose terminology only vaguely related to the world game and whose sense of pace failed to capture the rhythm of the sport. On television, where fewer words are often better, the feeling of many commentators, nevertheless, is that they are still obliged to "educate" the fan, creating a situation of talking down to some viewers and probably around some others.

The common link between what American writers and broadcasters are trying to achieve can be in the fact that "personality" still seems to dominate. The players are at the center of the reporting, more than the teams. Our media still concentrate on the big games and, inevitably, what the goal-scorer said or felt. The knowledgable European might pick out a midfielder as the most influential man in a match or cite a defender as the hub of the squad, but that presupposes an audience steeped in the game. For the American writer there is much to be learned by studying the Old Continent's treatment of the sport, but there is still the problem of finding his own audience and, at the same time, maintaining a critical view of the game and the people playing it.

The American writer and broadcaster at least have no shortage of models, nor any need to be reticent about seeking instruction. While it is not likely that the reporter here will ever be the "fan" or "critic" in the European sense, we can contribute something to the lexicon of the game, even if it is only to incorporate the traditions and values of other cultures into our own evaluation of the sport.

4.

The World Class Player—
What Makes Him Tick

Gerd Mueller, bearded, stocky, and surprisingly short, legs tree-trunk thick, stood in a corner of the Fort Lauderdale dressing room at Schaefer Stadium on an April afternoon and smiled quizzically when asked to describe an "offside" goal he had scored earlier in the afternoon. He struggled in German, his words translated by a mate, to offer the information that "the ball came off the post to me and it wasn't offside." Hardly illuminating data.

Down the room some 15 yards stood Teofilo Cubillas, star of two Peruvian World Cup bids, now the main scoring threat for Lauderdale, a team with high ambitions in the NASL. Thinner than Mueller, giving the impression of quickness and coiled power rather than brute strength, Cubillas admits that he is happier playing a midfield role than a winger's position, but can offer nothing of a memorable nature to encapsulate his performance that day.

Then there was the next afternoon in New Jersey, when Vladislav Bogicevic was inserted into the lineup at half time and helped turn a dour New York Cosmos team into an effective machine that gained a 4 to 2 triumph. Afterward, an enterprising questioner wanted to know what the Yugoslav World Cup man might have "learned" while watching the first half from the sidelines, what gems of knowledge were acquired that allowed Bogicevic to turn Tampa Bay inside out after intermission: "If somebody knows the game he already knows it," came the reply, short, to the point. "If he doesn't know the game, he'll never know it from the bench. I don't watch the game on the bench."

Or take Karl Heinz Granitza, the bullet-shooting West German forward who wears the uniform of the Chicago Sting. On a May night in Foxboro, Massachusetts, he smacked a 22-yard free kick to the top corner of the net with all the precision of a Wyatt Earp. How did he do it? "Maybe it's a lucky goal," he said. "I did the same against California. It's just a shooting goal. I hit it as hard as I can and the ball moves very fast." Did he aim for a spot? "No." So much for expecting the story of a carefully rehearsed execution.

Indeed, something that characterizes the greats of the game is often their inability to explain just what it is that they do so well, an argument for instinct or pure talent as factors of disproportionate importance. Of course the stars practice a great deal, the stories repeating themselves in essence: The really good ones always seemed to have a ball at their feet, played in the streets and fields from the earliest age, managed to find a spot to practice when others were already home for supper or attending to some other pursuits. That is the needed apprenticeship, but there are a thousand workmen for every one of the true artists.

Mueller, for instance, is the embodiment of the goalscorer, the man for whom every movement seems calculated to lead to something important. The most feared scorer in the world during his West German national team days, he remained so dangerous in the twilight of his career that he carried at least a two-man "escort" every step he took on a North American League pitch. Yet he beat that marking to score goals, beat it by repeating the same moves so regularly that they slowly washed away the defender's concentration. Caught offside once, Mueller was caught offside another ten times, always willing to gamble that the extra, quick step toward the ball would one time punish a defender who was a second too slow to spring the trap. Or he could receive the ball with his back to goal, his bulk and those huge thighs making him almost impossible to push out of position. Then he would feint, turn, and shoot, most likely frustrated by an agile defender or a quick goalkeeper, but, persistence again its own reward, often enough deceiving all with the idea and angle of the shot to score yet again.

But even seeing Mueller do it does not make it easy to describe what he does. In simple terms, he receives a soccer ball just fractionally onside and shoots it past an advancing goalkeeper, or he takes a pass low down, back to goal, turns and scores. It seems simple enough, is deceptively easy to relate in sentences, yet the statistics that collate the achievements and the words or pictures that describe his play miss the items that make it exceptional. All soccer fans have an indelible image of his winning goal against England in that epic 1970 León quarterfinal, head up, right foot high in the air across his body, left foot angled down for support as he returns to earth after propelling home the Jurgen Grabowski cross. Yet the picture only tells the end result, as the description of Mueller only suggests his goals. Getting to the ball in the first place, instinctively knowing where to be and what to do is what marks the classic scorer. Why did he run left instead of right? Why volley the ball instead of playing it on the short hop? Why attempt a difficult scissors kick when a flying header might have been logical? These are questions that the great scorers don't offer answers for. Instead, they so often say, "It was there and I did it without really thinking about it," and that must suffice for explanation.

Like many South Americans, Cubillas is noted as a free-kick expert, a label belying the fluidity of his total game, one based on quick acceleration and close ball control, a combination of abilities that allow him to round defenders and torment goalkeepers from the narrowest of angles. He is still extremely dangerous at the set pieces, still able to pick the top corners with 25-yard free kicks that seem to bend in the air and leave goalkeepers grasping sky, but he can cause as much havoc with his thinking and passing as with that thunderous left foot. Like many top players, Cubillas seems to have the instinct for the perfect pass, made over long distance at acute angles. It is a facet of the sport not easily appreciated on television, since the moment of the pass is often well before the time when the receiver is in position, hence the delivery of the 40-yard lead is based only partially on experience, the other part purely creative. You can see it happen from high above the field of play, but the television camera often only shows passer and receiver, leaving unknown the thought that made the movement.

Top class soccer produces action of a kind that is not easily explained in postgame analysis, not the kind of entertainment that is enhanced by knowing what the goal-scorer felt when he tallied. Rather it is the excitement and pleasure born of seeing something essentially abstract become a recognizable shape, a thing that apparently defies prediction and order achieving a type of inevitability and structure. Soccer is not a haphazard collection of errors that sometimes combine to achieve success. It is more often planned than unplanned, the creative moment more likely to be the result of thought than pure luck. What appears to be spontaneous is sometimes coordinated by a collection of minds. Even a relatively young player will sense these moments when the eleven men have one personality. They may be outgrowths of preparation and practice, coaching, and the refinement of team tactics, but the times when the game achieves its very best are likely to be those when something beyond mere planning has joined all the preparation.

Because these high moments are rare, it should come as no surprise that some of the men at the center of teams able to achieve that kind of understanding and production are rare, intelligent, impressive people, men whose presence is strong and whose humility is in marked contrast to the usual image of stars. That is not to say that a large ego isn't likely necessary for the achievement of individual brilliance, but to suggest that there is always the necessity to fit into the unit, no matter how superb the skills of the great player.

The North American fan has been remarkably fortunate in the early years of its professional game. Beginning with Pelé, the man whose very name became the basis of a league's viability, there have been a succession of top talents on view in NASL stadiums. Some of them, to be sure, have been the individualist for whom a team setting has always looked restrictive. Some have been past the peak of their powers, some merely tired of the adulation and daily pressures where soccer is religion and privacy unknown, but most have been lifted by their own pride to display the delicate wares that earned them fame in other settings. Most returned good value for money. The presence of the stars in the United States generates the publicity necessary to keep the sport going. The start of each new season is accompanied by the media barrages which announce the acquisition of a Klaus Toppmoller, Johan Cruyff, Rob Rensenbrink or Rudi Krol. The headlines serve notice that soccer in the United States is attracting men of world class at just the moment when its own roots are taking hold with a crop of young players about to break through to the professional level.

Soccer in North America turned on its first true star, Pelé, who came in 1975 and gave instant recognition to the game. It is difficult to recall the scenes that accompanied his arrival, so quick has been the sport's transformation, but the days that followed that hectic press conference to announce his signing were full of incident. Remember that first game Pelé played? It was an exhibition against Dallas, staged at faded Downing Stadium on Randalls Island in New York City, carried on national television on a Sunday afternoon. Pelé, of course, scored a goal, ever the dramatist ready to produce the needed conclusion.

The first league game the great man played was the following midweek, again at Downing Stadium, again to a capacity audience. The souvenir sellers were now fully armed and ready for the fans with flags of Brazil, pictures of Pelé, and hastily-acquired pennants—all available to the arriving multitudes. This was long before the NASL merchandised all of its wares in the now thoroughly professional manner. The fans parked where they could, some walking across the 125th Street bridge because that was as close as they could get to a stadium that once housed an Olympic Games trials but now was hardly the stage for a jewel's exhibition. There were no Pelé goals that night against Toronto, but the NASL proved what it had long felt. Given the attraction (the big name that is synonymous with sporting success in the United States), the public would come, even for soccer. Those jaded observers who had seen other temporary moments of enthusiasm for soccer, who had spent their careers standing in open fields covering matches between teams that hardly anybody ever heard of, were caught up in the fever of the time but unable to assess its meaning quite so soon.

Sports writers, of course, are sometimes fans who get paid for watching what they grew up adoring, but the men and women who daily assess the activities of teams and players can become hardened to the grind. Probably, at some point, we begin to regard sport as a job and the viewing of games as a business. If this is true for writers, whose presence is peripheral, never in the center of idolatrous autograph seekers, think what it must have been like for Edson Arantes do Nascimento, his face and legs known in even the most remote part of the globe by the single name, Pelé, instantly recognizable anywhere that radio, television, or rumor had ever reached. It is against this background of unnatural attention that his three years of competitive soccer in North America have to be measured. It was in this goldfish bowl atmosphere that the great man came to Hartford in 1975, his first season ending with injury so that he could make only a personal appearance at the match after carrying out his "press conference" duties the day before.

The Hartford team's games were being carried on local cable television that year and arrangements had been made to conduct an interview with him. Somebody must have thought that the audience was large enough to command 15 minutes of his time and it fell to me, a fledgling announcer who had gained the commentary task somewhat by accident, to meet the world's finest player in a specially lighted hotel room shortly after 6 P.M. This was after his full-scale meeting with the press, so there was an hour to watch him with all of the media, to try to formulate some questions that might not be exactly new, but maybe wouldn't be absolute replicas of the million he must already have answered around the globe. It would be nerve-wracking time too, because there could be no denying the fact that any soccer follower regarded Pelé as a legend and the opportunity to speak with him was unexpected. At the time the main fear was that I would lapse into spellbound silence and wind up with 15 minutes of Pelé's omnipresent smile for the halftime interlude the next night. Is it normal for reporters to be awed by the stars they work with? I think not. The interview with Pelé was unusual in that respect but he had played no ordinary role in sporting history and it is still something of a miracle that his career ended in places like Connecticut and Minnesota. Is it too much to suggest that his appearances had a regal nature? That he toured the world like an ambassador?

He came through the hotel room door at shortly after six, a shorter man than he looked behind a podium or on a playing field, the smile already gleaming. He was accompanied by his interpreter and friend, Professor Julio Mazzei, who eventually wound up as Cosmos's head coach. The three of us sat on a couch, ready to reenact a routine that was Pelé's NASL ritual, every city a sequence of press conference, television interview, game, press conference, then on to the next port of call. The questions went easily enough: "What is the nature of the injury?"; "Is it responding to treatment?"; "Will the Cosmos make the playoffs?"; "What about the quality of the NASL?" Pelé, through Mazzei, handled each easily and forthrightly, striking a lovely balance between candid sportsman and promotion-minded ambassador. He was flattering to his young American teammates, less positive about whether he would be able to get into a game before the playoffs, direct in saying that the Cosmos faced an uphill struggle to qualify. We were coming up with a matter-of-fact bit of halftime tape, the kind of thing you see every week. We had no real right to expect anything more.

During the course of the formal chat, I had been pleased to discover that I had almost no difficulty understanding Pelé's Portuguese, especially the soccer terminology. I suspect that it was a casual nod of the head or the manner in which one reacts to another's speech that indicated to him that I was comprehending his reply before Mazzei provided translation for the viewers. Slowly, he began to converse in a combination of

English, although he lacked confidence, of a very high quality, and Portuguese, while I tried a little of my own "Brazilian" dialect, which could not have sounded anywhere nearly as good as his use of my own tongue. During the next three-quarters of an hour, video equipment now being packed away, we chatted about the fact that his son Edson was learning English faster than his father, that there were some rising young stars in Brazil, a bit about soccer in North America, about the young players he had been impressed with in the NASL. It was all informal, no cameras, no notebooks out and I got the impression that Pelé enjoyed a bit of relaxation, didn't mind the fact that we often supplied one another with a missing word in whatever language combination was in use at the moment. He had the ability to make you relax, the facility of appearing completely interested in your own point of view. A most genuine, thoughtful man.

That was the first and last time I ever spoke with him or even asked a question at a news conference, though attending many more. (Indeed, I believe it was his last personal television interview until near his retirement, the Cosmos protecting his time more stringently in his next two years.) I felt I had been fortunate to be at the right spot for an hour when he was obviously not rushing to another engagement, on a night before a game that he was not to play in. Allowing that nobody "knows" anyone in an hour, I like to think that I saw some of him that evening, grasped a bit of his charisma. His moves on the field, his ability to predict the action, his organizational flair, sense of the dramatic—all of this must be the product of a personality of unusual depth and intensity. Soccer is not a game that can be fully organized. It must be influenced, and it was obvious that Pelé is a person of influence.

Pelé, of course, is not typical of the great stars in that his reputation and power is out of proportion to all others. When Franz Beckenbauer came to North America it would have been one hundred to one against many knowledgeable sports fans in New Orleans being able to tell you who he was and, even with all the publicity that the NASL has generated for its stars, not many have become "household" names. But the interesting thing about the truly great players I've observed is that all of them combine something of Pelé's self-assurance and creativity with their own particular brands of personality. Undoubtedly, the same could be true of dancers, artists, or opera singers, that all contain a central core of character and discipline that is integral to their act, but the transfer of characteristics across athletes isn't quite so easy to describe. Perhaps because the great soccer players are not American, hence do not readily fit our pattern of sporting self-importance, one is a bit surprised that they seem so much alike: After all, there are differences among nations and people. Those differences are reflected in the way soccer is played worldwide. Still, whether it be Pelé or Beckenbauer, Mueller, Cubillas or Giorgio Chinaglia, Bobby Moore or Giacomo Bulgarelli, there is a common strain to discuss.

Self-assurance and self-control seem most dominating, whether it is observed from a place on the terraces, a seat in the stands, or across the table at a press conference. These men project dominance, caused by their inner being, rather than by anything they may happen to do. On the field each may be demonstrative to a greater or lesser extent, a Chinaglia more obviously vocal than a Beckenbauer, but each is unquestionably a central figure. This centrality, however, does not lead to domination at the expense of team, perhaps because the game is harder to control than some others, more likely because their leadership and natural skill is brought forth from being the hub of the wheel, needing all of the spokes and rim in order to have full definition. Even their greatest achievements are part of a larger context, each man able to sacrifice his own golden skills for the unity of team or country, each able to develop the ability to remain ultra calm no matter how big the stakes. Self-assurance and self-control, the confidence that achievement is always possible, the discipline to see that the mind and body are tuned to that end: These characteristics mark these men's public faces.

Urbanity, too, radiates from them. If the definition of a gentleman is to be at home in any situation, then these world travelers have perfected the same skill without appearing markedly different from the crowds they entertain. One recalls Bulgarelli, brought into Hartford for the purpose of playing a couple of games as a guest star, seated at a luncheon table that was part of a remarkably strange atmosphere. Here was one of the world's great players (he had captained Italy, in fact, in the ill-fated World Cup of 1966, having been carried off hurt in that disastrous game against North Korea) willing to play games in North America because he, like many others, was intrigued by the growth of the U.S. game and wanted to make a contribution. Yet there were few writers present, those who were didn't quite know what to ask because it was uncertain what Bulgarelli's status was, and, to compound it all, the guest didn't speak English and the writers weren't fluent in Italian. Yet

Bulgarelli was relaxed, unruffled, a distinguished figure among others looking uncertain. If you had come into that room, searching for the man in charge, you would have moved toward that lean, handsome Italian.

Many of the greats have been professional players from their teenage days, few having had the benefits of higher education, with its ability to polish the rough edges; but it is sharply noticeable that these players didn't need such tutoring. It may be because the stars have traveled more, been placed in the international spotlight, but they acquire a certain amount of assurance, that ability to fit the demands of new surrounds. If they are not always able to articulate their own achievements, they are still thoughtful, disciplined in analysis, precise in conversation, intelligent in bearing.

I think of Bulgarelli, taking over a luncheon by his presence, in contrast to so many other players arranged at press conferences, their very bearing and look immediately suggesting that they were out of place, there to be displayed for a few moments before returning to the journeyman nature of the profession. The stars stand, sit, move differently, just as prima donnas are conscious of their importance and princes are aware of their place.

There is also an honesty about these men that can sometimes be misunderstood for self-esteem or arrogance, perhaps because of the aura surrounding U.S. sports stars. We tend to think our athletes should be humble even at the time they achieve their greatest moments. It may be one reason why athletes, when questioned after an important event, have so little to say. It could, of course, be that they have nothing to contribute, but I suspect that our playing heroes are a bit wary of being outspoken or appearing to be like everything and everybody. But great soccer players don't follow that credo, apparently secure in the knowledge and experience that their own sport is "criticized" in the sense of literature and music, rather than "reported" in the sense of American sports. It may come from the fact that these players have grown up expecting to read "reviews" of their performances the next day instead of mere accounts. Or it may be something common to all excellent leaders and people of unusual gifts: They are able to be brutally frank in self-evaluation and expect others to share such standards.

The urbane manner of the soccer star and its accompanying honesty combine to add another element to the design, that of the player's unusual ability to establish the pace of existence. Soccer is a game in which time operates as in life, simply coexisting with the action, 90 minutes an outline, an expectancy. There is the referee of course, but he doesn't ever really tell you what the rules are regarding time. The occasional hint ("You're wasting time, lad") is nothing more than hint and the ultimate reason for the length of a match is quixotic. In that environment, the ability to establish pace is a gift of the Gods.

Great players have it. They walk into a banquet room and immediately order the scene, actions occurring as they desire. It is incorrect to suggest that all great men give audiences rather than converse, but it is proper to recall that you are taking *their* time, not the other way round. On the field, these same stars are able to impose their exact rhythm and pace on the action. How many times has it been written that a Beckenbauer, a Bobby Moore, a Carlos Alberto always seems "to have more time to do things, to make the play" than do average players? In fact, it does not just seem that way. They *do* have more time than the average player. It is an eerie realization, one that sinks in when you sit high above the action and watch how understanding of the game, anticipation, and second sight allow the commanders of time to dictate to the enlisted men.

It is also the hardest facet of the sport for a new audience to fathom: the aspect of the game that is devalued in the popular indoor version. It is often not present at all in the scholastic or collegiate variety, where hustle and energy often replace vision and the ability to see two moves ahead. The control of time and pace is accomplished amidst constant movement, an ability that must mirror that of the racing driver who talks about being able to slow down the scenery at 200 miles per hour. The great players take the extra second to be certain of space, release the ball the split second before the defense closes down, move to the correct spot the second they are required to be there. It is more than timing involved, more than a practiced skill. It was clearly seen in context on a team like the New York Cosmos, where the cool quietness of Alberto, Beckenbauer, and Bogicevic served as foil for the constant running effort of a Ricky Davis, Johan Neeskens or Angelo DiBernardo. It is not a case of the stately being preferred to the energetic, but the recognition that some players can achieve more while appearing to exert less.

These men who dominate slowly share another characteristic: They are upright, formal in their bearing on the field. Beckenbauer's image is that of the straight back, foot poised over ball, the sweep of the leg, and the almost backward leaning cant to the body at the moment the pass is struck. "The Kaiser." Bogicevic is all square shoulders, head up, mentally searching for the opening while physically appearing to lope through the afternoon, a long stride deceiving by its ability to time the arrival to the precise instant when defender is beaten or advancing attackman dispossessed. "Mr. Control," says a friend with acute perception. Alberto, caressing the ball on the instep while attackers swarm around him, pirouetting before gently distributing the clearing pass, all done years after the "knowing" decided that his best days were long past and that Cosmos had acquired "reputation," not a player. What a misunderstanding of time that judgment was: There is still room for Alberto.

Soccer happens slowly enough so that there is time for thought, but accelerates so rapidly in the danger areas that much depends on reaction. That is where the classically gifted player, the one who drifts through the game like a ghost, has the ability to fascinate. How does an Alberto always seem to appear at the proper moment, yet so rarely there in a flurry of late sliding tackle or heaving effort that characterizes another defender launching himself at the last moment? They call it "reading the game" and the allusion to literature should not be filed and forgotten. Although soccer has no play book, it has a collection of possibilities and the finely-tuned player is constantly examining them with every movement. The dancer who perfects the moment of the leap is the player who measures the possibilities and gets them right.

This is not to overlook the contribution of the men whose conception of the sport is based on remarkable energy and the ability to channel that power and force at nearly constant pace. The image of Davis side-wheeling a goal in Los Angeles, of DiBernardo finding an additional gear to turn a defense, of Neeskens scything the air with his body as he dives to head a ball that no one else would reach, these are pictures of the game at speed, the finely-balanced contrast to the stately actions of their mates. Just as we admire those who have extra time to get the job accomplished, we marvel at the players who accelerate the game and still maintain control over their skills so as to be both fast and effective.

And control of pace and movement is the mark of the goal-scorer on that New York team, Giorgio Chinaglia. Perhaps because his round-shouldered, trundling movement made him appear slightly less elegant, perhaps because the fans misunderstand how many times a striker must be presented with opportunity before the real chance materializes, Chinaglia's acceptance by the fans was late in coming. Even as he was scoring goals with machinelike precision, his was the name most often hooted when announced, his mistakes greeted with derision, his goals with relief. He, too, marshals the game's pace by his positioning, his sprint to the ball, his constant battle with the defender to steal a step (really a *second*), before taking the opening that is present.

One benefit of the television replay is its ability to demonstrate just how fast everything happens at the moment of the scoring chance. The fan at the game sees the ball come through, the defender momentarily out of position. Chinaglia fastens onto the space and possession before picking his spot past a goalkeeper reduced to despairing dive or leap. That occurs in a flash, action contained in the smallest frame, with no chance at all for the shooter to be hesitant or imprecise. When the television tape is played back at a pace we mortals can live with, you can see that the decisions that made the difference were the outside of the boot, the flick of the heel, and the gentlest of pushes with the anchoring foot that set up the angle of the shot. Is it conscious effort? The unknowing might ascribe such tiny adjustments to luck, but the practitioner knows better even if he finds it difficult to describe the moment of decision. Chinaglia says he can remember every one of the goals he has scored, and there is no reason to doubt him. The artist knows the line that made the painting, just as the poet hears the language and sees the image. It is not chance.

Against that description of these men must be added an apparently obvious fact: They appear quite average. They could well have been grocers, postmen, factory workers; maybe would have been had it not been for this innate gift of playing an unusual game that demands a combination of high fitness, unique skills that are somewhat foreign to natural behavior, and the creative sense. Average, yes, in the sense that they are not likely very different from the fellows we sat next to in our school years, but surely different when it comes to translating the gifts they possess into their profession. It must be an incredible feeling to be able to perform something so well in the face of two great pressures: the knowledge that an opponent exists for the sole purpose of denying you that skill; and the fact that everything done is performed in public, before the inquiring, demanding, prying eyes of hundreds of thousands, all of whom possess a "certain" knowledge that they would do better if only they could do it at all. To succeed in the face of knowledge that an opponent is real and that envy demands your ultimate failure must give the highly competent performer a feeling of absolute strength.

Yet it is not strength in the sense of raw power that

these men demonstrate in conversation and appearance. It is that they are supremely in control. Perhaps it is all mask, a behavior adopted to hide the discomfort and uncertainty that might sometimes accompany the public career. But if it is a mask, it is worn with extreme ease. They look comfortable, even at the moment they communicate the fact that we are not all alike.

5.

Big Match Europe

The season doesn't explode but creeps into view. The occasional notices in the morning paper begin to shove aside the starting times for a myriad of golf tournaments. Soccer takes its place along with the word that raspberries are available for picking (bring your own containers) or that a tradesman is needed down the coast. Children run about the beaches in their football shirts. Soccer is about to return to Scotland after the summer break. Some professional teams cannot be certain, even, that all of their players will be immediately available, local holidays taking precedence for some of the part-timers who make up thirty of the country's thirty-eight clubs. Here in Scotland there are three divisions, eight clubs of which maintain fulltime staffs. Even some of the Premier League players might be part-timers, a situation unknown in American pro leagues.

As the preseason news seeps in, buried among horse racing predictions, snuggled alongside the weekend's cricket sides, you learn that St. Johnstone (First Division) is looking for a goalkeeper because its regular man has joined the police force in Aberdeen and cannot get to Perth for all the games; that there are so many players on holiday that Forfar (Second Division) is short reserves for its first preseason match; a player is sold from Dundee United to Hearts, but will still train in Dundee for a year because his studies aren't finished. That's the kind of accommodation commonly made in soccer over here, but it wouldn't be done that way in the U.S. would it? Reggie Jackson taking batting practice with the Red Sox because it was closer to his home? Tony Dorsett working out with the Giants all week, then playing for Dallas on Sunday?

Scotland is a small country that produces soccer players like some lands export precious minerals. The game sometimes seems enmeshed in Scotland's own traditions, its small cities and stadia restricting the outlook so that even as players head across the border or ocean in search of better wages and more acclaim, there seems only a vague sense of loss among the fans and writers, no sense of crisis among club directors and owners.

Scotland is no longer able to claim a world place except at the international level, its national team record markedly better in recent years than the performance of its teams in European club tournaments. The Scots have represented Great Britain in each of the last two World Cups and will be the first British country to ever play in three successive tournaments if they qualify for 1982s finals; yet their weekly soccer is not held in high esteem any longer. Continental teams don't quake when they draw Scottish opposition.

Still, there is one pairing in this country that may well surpass any in the world. It is a match of such passionate intensity that those who have never seen it cannot possibly imagine its atmosphere. It may, indeed, be the single unique sporting event, a confrontation that needs nothing special to fire its passion. Celtic versus Rangers is different, enthralling, dangerous, captivating. It never sneaks into view: It explodes.

Glasgow. A big, brawling, burly city, rebuilding, dynamic, vibrant. It emits vitality while simultaneously earning the reputation of the "hard man" of the country. It is a city of troubles, slums, and soccer fans who riot, but also the home of a marvelous art gallery, the Kelvin Hall, and a famous university. It lies tucked between the River Clyde and the western hills and isles, only forty-five minutes cross country from Edinburgh, but oceans away in reputation and respect. If Edinburgh, with its annual Festival, its graffiti in French and its historic link with Scotland's finest hours, is the jewel in the Old Kingdom's crown, Glasgow is the city that fights hard to escape second status, but still lives in the shadows. Its people sometimes distrusted by the more provincial, rural folk, and its byways awesome to the traveler from some tiny, distant place.

"Mind your wallet when you're in Glasgow," is the advice of one old-timer, as if the journey across country was a leap into another life. Glasgow is New York perceived from Des Moines: mythical, enticingly dangerous, clearly of questionable morality.

Scotland has few cities of great size, the country rural, broken by pockets of urbanity. Glasgow's million represents a fifth of the land's population and when one includes its influential economic role on the entire Southwestern Coast, maybe a third of the Scots are included in the heartbeat of their noncapital city. When unemployment hits Glasgow, it hits Scotland, but when it's boom time in Aberdeen, by contrast, the prosperity may be limited to the northeastern fringe, hardly touching other's hard times.

Glasgow is cut off from the rest of Scotland by its very role in the country; and it is split in half, itself, by religion and tradition. Is there a soccer fan alive who has not heard the story of Glasgow Rangers, the Protestant bastion, and Glasgow Celtic, the club that wears the Shamrock and whose fans wave the flag of the Irish Republic? For years it has been going on, more sharply focused today by the conflict in Ulster, just across the Irish Sea to the South. The issues transcend soccer, but it is soccer around which the volatile fans twist and turn, their behavior noticeable around the world because Celtic and Rangers not only carry those fans with them, but also completely dominate soccer in this country. You could forgive a mildly interested European for not knowing that there *are* other teams in Scotland, so regular is the "Old Firm's" participation in European tournaments. Glasgow isn't Scotland, but Glasgow is the heartbeat of Scotland's soccer, a one-two, Celtic-Rangers, Rangers-Celtic, that repeats daily, monthly, season after season.

Glasgow crowds aren't average, either. They are the gatherings that make Scotland's soccer known around the world by their intensity and sheer size, their emotional commitment to one team or the other outdistancing mere love and becoming fanaticism. When you sit at

Hampden Park and the two teams emerge from the tunnel for one of their confrontations, the old lady of a stadium shakes with energy and verve, the terracing a sea of color and a wall of noise, the football pitch an arena and the athletes gladiators, the stakes well beyond what normal mortals should be expected to fight for. You've heard the roar at other events: the exultation that greets a championship victory in any sport, the anticipation of excitement that builds before a match of large proportions. But you have not heard the roar of pure passion, the sounds that some label "pure hatred" until you've been at Celtic-Rangers at that moment when those two teams come onto the field for a match of soccer. The action that follows is always mirrored by the scenes and sounds around it, integral to the event but entirely the event.

Yet, on a pleasant, brilliantly sunny August afternoon, Glasgow hid its darker face. I arrived by train from Fife for a soccer session that would mean three matches within twenty-four hours, two of them at Rangers' home ground, Ibrox Park, the other the epic battle itself, a match between the giants for the preseason trophy called the Drybrough Cup. Supposedly the latter game should be called a "friendly" since no League points or national honors are at stake, but there isn't much evidence of friendly rivalry. Indeed, one of the local journalists characterizes their meetings as "Christians versus Lions, where they paw at each other from opposite ends of the stadium. It's pure bigotry, that's all it is." Maybe, but there is another life to it, an energy that demands examination. I knew it the minute I arrived at Ibrox on the perfect Friday night when a gentleman at the press door wanted to take a look inside my traveling bag before I was allowed up the stairs into the hallowed halls themselves.

"Got to look inside that bag before you go anywhere," he said jovially, not an unusual request in the United Kingdom at any time in the last decade. "The Stars and Stripes and IRA you know." As a matter of fact, I didn't, but the tote bag does have a tiny U.S. flag on it, a little traveler's patriotism.

"It's a sweater in case it turns cool later on," I replied in my best visitor's manner.

"Holy Water, you say?" came the reply.

Even allowing for the fact I don't speak English with a burr, I don't think I was misunderstood to that extent. Instead, I had been greeted immediately by an aspect of soccer life in Glasgow. It hit home sooner than I could have expected. There would be more, quite a bit more, before the next twenty-four hours were complete. The start of the second half of the preliminary match, for instance, was cue for Rangers supporters to begin their evening's concert. "Bring on the Rangers!", "When the 'Gers go Marching in" and other ditties had been interspersed with "God Save the Queen" and a tune that emphatically suggested, "Fuck the IRA." All this before the heroes of the night even made an appearance, and, don't forget, the songs were directed at an opponent who wasn't even on the card that night. What would somebody make of it, walking into a soccer stadium, hearing a group of people singing songs about the IRA, walking down the Glasgow streets after the game being followed by a gaggle of boys who suggest that the proper thing to do is "fuck the Pope," all messages conveyed at the top of their register? It should not mystify a student of history, but it surely cautions those who think that old distrust is dead and buried.

It is simplistic to say that the emotion that surrounds Celtic and Rangers is an extension of history, but British history cannot be escaped. There is irony in the fact that the once independent Kingdom of Scotland became part of the United Kingdom in 1707, over half a century before America became independent. The ultimate price of absorption was a catastrophic raid against the Catholic North in 1745. A last attempt to restore a Stuart monarchy to Scotland failed miserably at Culloden Moor and, on their way home, the invading English army laid waste to some of the Highlands. Had it ended then all might be different, but the 19th century saw famines in Catholic Ireland coupled with industrial growth in Britain, a return of many Irish to Scotland, and resulting divided populations in the major cities. Irony is perhaps not strong enough to describe the present scene: Having once been hunted down, the clansmen now find themselves the tourist symbol of Scotland, the kilts and bagpipes luring travelers from Europe and the Americas to see the traditional style of Scottish rural life. The stores are full of tartans and books on the clans and histories of the old days, but what can safely be revered at a historical distance is hardly welcomed when it spews forth at a soccer ground. When Rangers fans sing "God Save the Queen," it's a reminder that the Protestants ultimately proved the winner in a struggle of religion that was bitter, with a lingering aftermath.

The soccer history is almost as compelling. Although Rangers have publicly said they will hire Catholic players, diligent research by people in the know says they've had only a couple. Writers add that Rangers aren't showing any signs of changing a policy referred to here as "sectarian." Celtic, by contrast, rose to its greatest heights when managed by a Protestant, Jock Stein. But isn't it ridiculous that the religion of a team boss is known in this day and age? Yet, some Celtic supporters carry the flag of the Irish Republic to matches and nobody says that the Shamrock they proudly display is a symbol of the United Kingdom.

It goes deeper, too. You cannot attempt to understand centuries of history and a lifetime of feelings in a decade of regular visits to a country. You know that there are, effectively, separate school systems for Protestants and Catholics in Glasgow. You can understand that there are, effectively, separate pubs and neighborhoods. You can see that nobody is truly neutral in his attitude to the teams. Even the people who claim no interest in, no experience of, soccer, the prim ladies you speak with, while dissociating themselves immediately from the clubs and the sport, have formed their opinions. Listen between the lines for a few minutes and you'll discern the fact that religious issues are very much alive in Scotland.

Under current scheduling practices, the archrivals play at least four times a year, twice at Ibrox and twice at Celtic Park, at the opposite end of the city. However, Cup competitions such as this preseason affair, the League Cup, the Scottish FA Cup, and the Glasgow Cup mean that they can clash much more than that. Cup finals are usually played at neutral Hampden Park, Scotland's aging national stadium. Such was the case this particular Saturday.

Hampden stands in the aura of its history. A huge red sandstone structure, the park is a semicircular block of terraces confronting a main stand. Much of the spectator space is open to the elements, while dirt parking areas must become quagmires in a typical winter. Even though these are the sights that greet you after turning into that innocuous little road which leads to one of the world's fabled stadiums, you still think of the one hundred and thirty-four thousand fans who have been jammed in to see Scotland-England or a Cup final in the distant past. This is the home of the "Hampden roar," that swelling adulation which greets Scottish sides and has been known to reduce experienced visitors to quaking performers. It is the scene of most of Scotland's great triumphs, the site of the legendary Old Firm Cup battles.

The ground actually belongs to a little amateur team, Queens Park FC, and you can inhale the tradition here, from the two towers that loom above the main stand, turretlike in their resolute silence, old, strangely echoing as you make the long climb from ground level to the press box and its vista of playing field and skyline beyond. Such tradition can be majestic as well as stifling. It is tradition, surely, that has lifted Scotland to its place in world soccer, so much higher than it ought logically to be. After all, this country was the smallest to qualify for the 1978 World Cup finals, yet nobody here seems to even consider that a remarkable fact. "Maybe we should think that getting to the finals is something," a reporter says, "but until we win it we won't really be satisfied." That attitude is what makes a small country achieve and makes for the atmosphere of Scottish soccer.

The exterior of the park is industrial Victorian, its surroundings residential and aged, but the interior is transformed by hordes of supporters. Rangers, to my left, the Celtic green and white to my right, the uncovered end of the ground. "Rangers always have that end," answers a writer when I ask who decides which group gets wet when it rains, so you score one for Rangers at the covered end or credit Celtic for always braving the elements.

Glasgow and the surrounding hills (it is, like Rome, a city on seven hills) are visible through the window created by the end of the side terraces directly opposite and the dip in the huge, high-banked terrace to my right, where the Celtic colors are waved and Celtic songs are sung. There is not the skyline view that you get at Ibrox, the crush of apartment buildings blocking too much of the panorama and unlike Wembley Stadium in London, with its roof extending much the way round, Hampden is open, so that the cauldron of sound develops low, escaping straight up and out instead of rebounding as it does in the English national stadium. But the sloping terraces here give the field of play even more of an arena feeling, the players almost straight beneath you as they emerge for battle.

What happens over the next 90 minutes cannot easily be portrayed in words any more than the natural world can be reduced to computer statistics. Just as the computer may stack numbers and permutations, the writer can stack the images, but the reader will not succeed in arranging them in exactly the manner that recaptures the mood and aura of those two 45-minute halves and its drama. Stack the images: the continual song, the noise that rises and falls with the action; the sea of color, every color, but predominantly blue-jerseyed Rangers with the big white numerals on their backs and the green-and-white stripes of Celtic, with the green numbers on their thighs; the ring of police who watch both ground and match; the stretcher bearers who are active throughout the afternoon as one fan or another succumbs to drink or heat or argument; the held breath as the action builds toward a shot, the release of tension that comes with the resultant effect, the explosions of sound that come when a goal is scored. There is nobody neutral here, nobody except the American.

Amidst all that, a Rangers defender named Sandy Jardine, one of the experienced men in his side, reinforced a fundamental notion as Rangers won, 3–1: despite all that surrounds the confrontation, the bad feelings and the bad publicity and the fear that many Scots have of going near one of these matches, it is the game that still transcends all that and it is the game that has the power to lure the best from players and spectators alike. This particular Saturday, Jardine gathered possession at his own 18-yard line midway through the opening half and stepped straight into memory.

Quickly he moved forward, past a stranded forward into the space that appeared between the halfway line and his own penalty area. Celtic had been cutting off Rangers near the centerfield region during this spell of light pressure, but Rangers had been guilty of releasing the ball too quickly, looking for Davey Cooper or John MacDonald out wide when they were too tightly marked to do anything with hard-won possession. Now Jardine eschewed the pass and elected to dribble the ball forward, carrying with him a pocket of space as defenders retreated in front of him to cut down his passing lanes. He was 80 yards from the Celtic goal and his burst represented no apparent danger.

Continental players do not carry the ball as much in this dribbling fashion when under pressure, but Scotland still likes to see the man in possession have a go at the defenders. Everybody seems to relish that moment of freedom when the ball is there and space opens in front. Jardine now rushed forward. Celtic had its chance to stop the attempt. What was required was a decisive intervention, an acceptance of the relative importance of the situation, and the action required to balance it. Three Celts knew it, converging on the Rangers' man at the center circle, waiting to greet him and stop the solo dash. Two came from the front, approaching at speed from defensive positions, while a third came from the rear, recovering from the attack's loss of possession to enter what had now become, for him, a pursuit. The rest of the defense was stretched wide across the field for it must not be forgotten that other Rangers were chasing into positions to receive the expected pass, were drawing men away from Jardine's area by their runs. All of them, surely, knew at the next moment that the white ball would be launched in their direction, so their actions were not subterfuge to confuse an experienced group of backliners.

Jardine carried forward, meeting the three-man challenge at the white center line, halfway between the screaming Celtic fans at his back, still oceans away from that sea of his own supporters who stood ready to greet his eventual arrival. There was a clash of bodies, four men around one white ball and the referee not far away, either. Perhaps there was a hint of a foul. Maybe somebody in the defense thought there would be a whistle, maybe there was the tiniest of pauses, the collective moment when nobody actually made the necessary commitment to stop the action. In that second the pattern formed, coalesced, then opened again with Jardine running free toward the Celtic goal, the ball still at his feet.

Certainly now the pass would come, the defense outnumbered, Jardine's midfield magic having won the day. The back veered to his right, still pressing forward, ignoring Cooper wide out one side and some other blue shirt away out on the other. There was one challenge left, in the form of Celtic defender Danny McGrain, who now came from his own 18-yard line to confront this man who had swept some 60 yards but needed another few steps before a shot could materialize. Having angled so far to his right, the ball fractionally in front of him, always where he could flick it away from a challenge, Jardine now seemed to be taking himself away from the face of the arena, away from the challenging shot, perhaps readying for the telling moment when someone would hew off behind him, racing the opposite diagonal to leave the last line of defense no chance to adjust, to make goalkeeper and defenders commit themselves. As that was shaping to occur, McGrain was advancing, his bearded face clearly recognizable and the final confrontation about to be played out.

The last decision is the one that transformed the afternoon. Jardine cut sharply left, dragging the ball from right to left boot and stranding McGrain in the process. Now keeper Bob Latchford faced the moment and could only come hurtling off his line, vainly because the Ranger had the time, space, and patience to pick his spot, low to Latchford's left hand side. The Celtic keeper went down, but went down in response to what had already happened. He was a character in a scripted drama at that moment, no alternative but to accept defeat.

There was, as always there is in these events, the time when, just before the shot came in, silence made its presence known. Just as you slow the journey down in your mind's eye, see every move that Jardine made, imagine the twists and turns and recall the way his shoulders were hunched forward and his head nodded slightly to the right, you can stop the event at the moment the shot came in, when it was apparent that this run of 80 miraculous yards, through what amounted to a whole team's defense, was going to result in a goal. When you stop at that moment there is no noise. The match took place in a cauldron, but wasn't that silence just before Jardine shot? The event requires rewriting if it were not the case.

No, it is not all pleasant to be among those masses of people who care so much, *too* much about winning and losing and all of the side issues; it is not pure fun to spend an afternoon wondering when the pot will boil over, whether there will be ugly scenes to mar the enjoyment of the game. It will not always be the case, too, that there will be a moment to lift the game as dramatically as did Jardine's run and goal in the 28th minute on the first Saturday of August 1979, but you suspect that within the context of this match, at the epicenter of that drama, there always exists the possibility because the heroes rise to the moment of confrontation and even the very young players gain age and wisdom in the setting.

The terraces, which had only forty-five minutes before been choked with singing, stomping fans, were empty concrete grey and white by 5:30 P.M., not even the lone sweeper to raise an echo against the occasional sound of a telephone's ring, speaker's burr, or tea cup's clink, in a press box high above them. The drive back to Glasgow was uneventful, the streets empty of fans and no team colors to be seen. The fans had largely come on foot or by public transport and they went home that way, Rangers to the left, Celtic to the right as they had come. It is a world of its own, as inexplicable as America's own sporting classics, but the big crowd is the life blood of the sport, the vehicle that raises sport from mere physical action toward an objective to true theater. When you see good teams before smallish crowds (and that is often the case both home and abroad), there may be time to be reflective, to marvel at the technique, to appreciate the subtle touches, but when forty thousand make a stadium into a choirloft and the event takes place in constant sound, which seems to lend purpose to even meaningless events, then you have an entirely new facade. Soccer takes on its most exciting form when there is that huge, passionate group of onlookers, because it is a game of such shifting fortune that it revels in the uncertainty of it all. You so often come close to doing things right, so rarely get them exactly right: can there be greater satisfaction than to get it right and then have this kind of choir sing your praises?

Of course, this crowd is a crowd that cares terribly about winning and losing. It is not a forty thousand that has come to be "entertained," not forty thousand people at least half of whom have come for the hot dogs, the beer, and the day out. It is not ten thousand families on outings, tailgating in a parking lot. It is forty thousand people who chose sides long ago and now come to see their favorites prevail. It will be twenty thousand winners and twenty thousand losers and there will be gloating in victory, suffering in defeat, not always in silence. It is the passion that lifts the sport, the hardest element to engender in a growing game in the New World. We still must recognize that many of our large American crowds come to see the stars or for the "entertainment," prepared not to care vitally about the result. We can even say, "That's good," because the passion for winning most certainly contributes to the problems of crowd control that plague the game across the world.

But to remove that passion is to fundamentally change the game.

The critics overseas may contend that the youths are damned, that society is falling apart, but nobody can deny that a soccer crowd cares passionately about something in an age when apathy is often put forward as a major problem. These people cared about the result, they are already savoring it if they were for Rangers, plotting revenge in the next match if they are Celtic men. Happily, there was no crowd problem to mar the scene, but nine months later that would not be the case; mounted police charged the spectators who fought on the field at the end of the 1980 Scottish Cup final game.

Putting Celtic-Rangers in a context is difficult, if not impossible. The teams are larger than Scottish soccer life, the fans as much of the match as the players. Such is the passion of the two groups that Celtic and Rangers are guaranteed thirty-four "home" matches a season in Scotland, because wherever they go they are greeted by loyal legions. The same fellow who sported the tangerine of Dundee United last Saturday, stood on the terraces near you, may show up next week in green-and-white if Celtic is the visitor. The man who cares about every Cowdenbeath result may also be a Rangers supporter and will show up in red, white, and blue if the 'Gers ever come to Central Park for a Cup match.

It is more than sport, this kind of intense following, but it is the reason why the teams attract such attention. Thousands of miles away, on that snowy morning in New England when the BBC announcer simply reports the scoreline, "Celtic 0, Rangers 0," there must be more than one expatriate Scot who knows that it was more than a mere result.

6.

The English Game

There are magic names in English soccer, teams, stadia, players that serve to define the sport for fans across the globe. There is a satisfying ring to the collection of names that appear in the list of the ninety-two clubs, so many having been transplanted to other parts of the world during the days of Empire. There is a nod of acknowledgement from even the casual follower of the sport when the great London teams are mentioned, Newcastle United is pronounced or Wolverhampton Wanderers is spoken. But the names that mean the most are Arsenal, Liverpool, and Manchester United, Wembley, Old Trafford, and Anfield Road, Sir Matt Busby, Herbert Chapman, and Bill Shankly.

Wembley has always been at the center of English soccer, or at least it seems that way. Built in 1923, the great white edifice with its twin towers is probably the best-known stadium in the world, site of the 1966 World Cup final and over fifty Football Association Cup finals. Even the Midwestern American has seen it captured from the television lens as a helicopter circles above its seats and terraces, partially roofed, nearly one hundred thousand fans packed inside to savor an upcoming soccer or rugby match. To be inside is to hear a deafening cacophony, smashing waves of noise, which hit that metal roof and circulate back onto the very singers who lifted the chant to begin with. To sit high above the emerald green surface, known for a texture that saps the strength from nervous players' legs, is to enter a soccer world where one speaks in hushed tones if only so as to not betray the newcomer's nerves.

Arsenal was the English League team that dominated between the wars, the era when the game moved from its limited British perspective to a world stage, and the Gunners (as they are nicknamed) of North London have maintained their place in the sport with a record of unparalleled excellence. Never relegated from the First Division, Arsenal is a side against which others measure themselves, a team whose reputation is worldwide. The man who runs the souvenir shop attached to Highbury Stadium ticks off the places he regularly mails programs to and recalls the faces and dress of visitors from Kansas to Kenya.

Herbert Chapman was the manager who directed Arsenal in its glory days of the 30s, an innovator who made a basic change in formation to take advantage of his great talent and emphasize the power game in the center of the field, something that is now an English trademark. Busby survived the Munich air disaster to lead

Manchester United to its greatest win, the capture of the European Cup in 1968, the evening when English soccer finally escaped a shadow and proved itself equal to the best on the Continent. Shankly constructed the heart of the Liverpool side that was to stride across English football in the 70s to salvage a faltering reputation for the national sport when it was so badly needed.

No fan of the world's game has not heard of these teams, these men or the fabled places of the game in England. Even though Rangers versus Celtic is unique, a combination of circumstances that creates something the traveler must sample, the roots of the world game are in the South, emerging continental powers merely extensions of the game's heartbeat. They talk now of the West German crowds singing in unison "in the English style"; they speak of the marvelous stadiums of Spain, Italy, and Portugal, and of the atmosphere of the big matches in all of the lands. But discussion of soccer tradition always returns to England and to the industrial North or that London stadium near the Arsenal Underground stop.

There is something of the New York Yankees about Arsenal, the big city team that plays with a slight swagger, with the knowledge that it belongs among the elite even if the current record suggests otherwise. Highbury is a giant yet cozy arena in which to see a game, its crowd clearly cultured and polished, the team on display always tactically correct, if sometimes unadventurous. Like the cautious stockbroker who may go to see the Gunners play, the team will not gamble on the spectacular if planning and execution of the percentages will bear similar fruit. Maybe that is why Arsenal has been so effective over the years. The expectation that it will turn out right in the end usually means that Highbury Hill is the scene of celebration in League, Cup, or League Cup action for most of the season. No one has made the trip to Wembley for an FA Cup final as many times as Arsenal (11) and only Newcastle, Blackburn Rovers, and Aston Villa have won the trophy more often, but none of them in the past twenty-five years. The tournament was first staged in 1871, time enough for reputations to have been created.

Soccer in London has its own mood, its own sophistication, such that the followers of the game in Britain say you have to get away from Westminster, out to Birmingham, Leeds, Newcastle, and Sunderland to sample its flavor there, off to the smaller, "homier" clubs like Southampton, Ipswich, and Coventry to taste their vintage before you will catch all of the reflections of the sport. But the international fan will want a ticket to Anfield Road and Old Trafford to complement the look at Highbury, the taste of the Kop in Liverpool, and the Stretford Road End in Manchester anticipatory even before the first English breakfast is properly digested.

Anfield is the home of Liverpool, most successful side in England this past decade, king of Europe on three occasions, reviver of faith in a flagging English game. Old Trafford houses Manchester United, the team with the worldwide following, partly built on a tragic Munich night of 1958, but reinforced by two decades of inventive, exciting soccer that has contained almost equal elements of achievement and disappointment.

English soccer is back at its high level, perhaps a response to renewed prestige and performance of the national team, but just recently the sport was in trouble. The 1974 World Cup, the 1976 European Championship, and the 1978 World Cup qualifying were all flunked. Not since 1970 had England gone onto an international soccer field with heads truly high and the effect on the domestic game in the mid-70s had been apparent: The press was castigating a lack of skills, comparing the natives in uncomplimentary terms with European and Latin American rivals. But all that has changed now that the 1980s have begun. Liverpool twice won the European Cup and Nottingham Forest made it four in a row for England with success in 1979 and 1980. The national team qualified for the European finals and is on the way to respectability again.

I suspect that there is much about the playing of games that involves the manner in which they are thought. Players attempt only the possible and the possible is determined by available examples. As the English regain their self-image, as the ignominy of 1974, 1976, and 1978 is replaced by the feats of Liverpool and Forest and England, there is a revival of spirit. Yankee Stadium has those plaques in centerfield to recall the heroes of old; English soccer has Anfield and Old Trafford, fabled for their sounds, not looks, compounded of team success and fan vibrance. They are alluring places as you head for the English game.

The clippers once sailed from Liverpool's ports before steam changed the way of life and again today it is a thriving, modern city, one whose central square is dominated strikingly by the St. George Hall, the Walker Art Gallery, and the Nelson Monument, all rising away from the Mersey, the great river port that names the whole region. England looks and feels different from Scotland, the towns bigger and more spread out, the row houses with their characteristic chimney stacks flashing by train windows. It is world apart in soccer, too, its huge population centers supporting teams on a scale that is the equal of America's top major leagues.

Liverpool has become the byword for measuring perfection in English soccer, building its reputation on a succession of stunning achievements in Europe while making the domestic scene almost its own. The saga began under the lead of Shankly and has been carried on without break by Bob Paisley and its soccer is international in scope, tops in individual achievement. The honors have included everything that can fall to an English club plus more than one hundred matches in the Continental tournaments.

Yet there is nothing about the approach to Anfield that suggests all of the majesty housed inside. The Liverpool stadium is reached by the Everton Road as you sweep out from the central area, a right turn past the *Spion Kop* (also the nickname of the fabled ground's end) pub, into a thoroughfare clogged with fans even an hour before the match, bringing the final approach, now red and white and alive. The vendors with their scarves and favors, the fish-and-chips shops vying for patronage with the pubs and program sellers emphasize that you are in football territory, even if the ground, less than a block away, is still not visible, tucked down a side street where only a massive iron gate indicates that you are near hallowed territory.

Red is the Liverpool color and red the color of Anfield. Red seats and scarves, shirts and hats, even a red sky that will soon turn black and produce driving rain and a lovely rainbow simultaneously. There is the Kop on your right, the terraces on which stand the Liverpool youngsters, chanting, singing, and waving their flags as the season is about to begin. As this is 1979–80 opening night, the 1978–79 championship trophy is paraded before the start of the match, letting the faithful see tangible evidence of success on the field. Like some holy relic, the golden cup is carried between two uniformed boys who make a complete circuit of the pitch, the crowd leaning forward at each point to catch a glimpse of the trophy, rising as one man to salute this 20th-Century version of a saint's bones. The ritual continues when Liverpool appears, the players loping to the center circle to wave greeting to all corners before setting off for a last five minutes' preparation before play. As the men disperse for their own last moments of thought they participate in a singsong ritual, each player's name lovingly chanted by the Kop until the designated hero turns, gives a two-handed wave to acknowledge the adoration, then resumes his privacy.

What is it that makes tradition? It is far more than simple results, for there are successful teams in many sports that don't play their way into the hearts of supporters. I suspect that the tradition of a Liverpool is like that of the Montreal Canadiens, compounded equally of a desire for perfection in performance and that ability to attain something like emerald quality often enough to suggest that diamonds are possible. As Montreal fans disdain the average and complain when mere results are substituted for gems, the Liverpool crowd adopts the same love-hate attitude toward the game that is evident this night, happy when their heroes demonstrate the subtle touch that marks them artists, disappointed ultimately when all of the invention fails to produce a goal against a Bolton Wanderers side that came to put up the shutters and achieve a 0–0 result. Liverpool rarely fails to break down such packed defenses, tactics they have come to know as part of the price of high achievement and reputation. But tonight their shooting is just that shade inaccurate and good fortune eludes them at the crucial moments. But there is far more than the result. Everything about Liverpool is big time, the program thirty-two pages long and filled with information, the public address system informative and easily understood. The ushers are present and visible and the atmosphere is geared for fun and achievement. No exploding scoreboards, of course, but Liverpool is a great club in the latest modern way: They take the field with HITACHI etched across their shirts, the Oriental electronics firm that is their new sponsor, perhaps merely the tip of a big business iceberg about to lift British soccer. Those delightful fans, the ones who give Anfield its special sound, are more like Americans than any I've seen in Britain. Apparently affluent, families come for a good time, for the souvenirs, to be part of the success story, make the evening pleasant if not spectacular.

The walk away from the ground is into a cool, bracing evening, the streaks of light in the sky blending with street lights and traffic moving in the distance. Some forty thousand nine hundred have been on hand but they disperse remarkably quickly. Within thirty minutes, save for the fact that the pubs around the ground are humming with activity, you would not have known there had been a match. This city, which presents its industrial face from the train windows but displays a Michelangelo in its art gallery, is quickly back about its business, content to display sophistication, aware that the world runs on industry and trade. And football.

Like Liverpool, Manchester has it own face to display

twenty-four hours later. The cities, indeed, are sisters, a bare forty-eight minutes apart by train from Lime Street to Victoria, a ride that takes you across country, through suburbs and the occasional open area, never quite attracting the eye with a spectacular vista. It had been apparent that England was growing like megalopolis of home, but today reinforces the notion with a caveat that is refreshing: Despite the absence of true countryside, the heavily populated region still has space for parks and playing fields and patches of open area, even if the most catching scenes are the paved town squares that dominate both Victorian cities. Liverpool has its massive hall, Manchester an Albert Square, overlooked by a striking Victorian building that now does service for a myriad of city functions.

Manchester, too, is more pristine than its neighbor, a city where finding a hotel is uncharacteristically hard, a place of spanking storefronts, hugh offices, and an unending row of banks. It looked all business this Wednesday afternoon, professional and polished, putting its best face on a day when the sky dripped rain and did its utmost to convert the scene to wash. There was not the bustle of New York, not the elbows-out, keep-moving-ahead attitude of Fifth Avenue at noon, but Manchester is a city moving, people heading from here to there. Twentieth-century workday, but also the city of the Free Trade Hall where Mrs. Pankhurst spoke in support of woman's suffrage, home of the Hallé Orchestra, one of the world's great musical groups. Culture reaches out and touches the casual walker in Manchester, architecture reminding of the Victorian Age design even as the bustle and sheen of commercial edifices suggest a new era.

History, too, is part of Manchester United, a side linked forever to a night in West Germany when the heart of a team, regarded as the best in England, so marvelously young, was stilled in a plane crash in bad weather. Dead were many of the stars of the side as well as reporters who had traveled with them. Badly injured was manager Matt Busby, later to be knighted for his services to soccer. There is a clock at Old Trafford that remains forever set at that tragic moment of the crash. It took ten years for United to come all the way back to the top, ten years in which they discovered and nurtured some of the great stars: George Best, Bobby Charlton, and Denis Law are three of the memorable ones.

It was the air crash, certainly, that transformed United from a well-known English team into the "Notre Dame" of world soccer. Other teams have suffered horribly in disasters, but none gathered anything like United's following as a result. The current side has supporter's clubs in remote spots, vicarious followers every time they take the pitch, but even the knowledge that millions care about the outcome cannot add much to the feeling that strikes a United player when he steps on field at home, greeted by those fifty-five thousand fanatics who come in person to worship at the game's shrine. They line up outside the main gate, a gaggle of people stretching for half a mile, stand there in a downpour of rain or tepid sunshine, prodded into position by the omnipresent mounted police, red-and-white-and-black striped scarves the predominant color of the scene.

This is the Manchester United crowd, a following that is feared through the United Kingdom and Europe because its very size has provided anonymity for hooligans who prefer a Saturday afternoon fight to a soccer game, a crowd that is always huge, always passionate in support of its heroes. The Stretford end, to your left when you sit in the main stand press box, is the traditional gathering place of the truly committed, the noise makers of United who greet friend and foe with sonic energy, whose staccato sets the tempo for the match. The terraces opposite Stretford are equally jammed with United support, all of the standees caged in by brightly-red-painted iron bars, tops swept back to form pikes to discourage any who would be so foolhardy as to attempt to rush forward. Neatly pinned in by further fencing and gates, the faithful are in their places an hour before kickoff, ready for the night's entertainment, content to sing their lungs out. You will, however, be reminded of this crowd's darker side at the end of the match.

Tonight powerful, noisier, less sedate than Anfield, bordering on kinetic, Old Trafford rocks when the game begins and the players seem to take their cues from the turbulence. Visitors, surely even hardened professionals, must find the game a nervy affair, especially two West Bromwich Albion men who have done previous service with the other team in Manchester, City. This night they are subjected to an unmerciful taunting, whether it be the "happy" cry of "Hello, hello, City rejects" or the whistling of shrill intensity that greets their attempts to take a free kick or corner with precision. It is the kind of pressure that must boil up inside a player, the athlete knowing that the only way to turn off the tap of noise is by scoring, the very difficulty of that reply increased manifold times by the occasion's tension. United players, too, seem influenced by the wall of song and the bursts of enthusiasm that greet the well-judged pass or the well-made tackle: Indeed, United achievement is explosive noise, craters carved in the sky by the unity of voices that raise their cadence for the instant it takes to acknowledge success.

Given two goals, one early in each half, United wins in a manner that is workmanlike, not especially vivid. What the home side did best was to ride the wave, gathering force and power as the game progressed, gradually grinding Albion out of the action and substituting its own persistence in attack for the smooth stuff that others can offer. As United gathered power over the last 45 minutes, the clouds drifted in from the Stretford end, low, nearly atop the stand and an eerie, reflective cloud hovered just off center in the line of vision. It combined to suggest a Shakespearean atmosphere of devastation and destruction for the visitors, grimly defending the end that was now backdropped by the elements and attacked by a force of incessant power in red and white.

If Liverpool is like Montreal's search for perfection and the socially acceptable, Manchester United strikes a visitor as the more vibrant, harder environment. Those fans who waited in those interminable lines before the match are passionate ones who come ready to cheer their heroes, not the opponent. Yes, there was the occasional burst of applause for a well-executed Albion attempt, but this was sport in which the idea was to win and the fans were there to reward success. Maybe that is why United has been so powerful in Cup competitions. Given this kind of following they must strike fear into everyone in one-day action.

That passion dissipates quickly after a match ends.

Having gathered as early as 6:30 P.M., the Stretford crowd departs like a waterfall and that end is absolutely empty twelve minutes after the final whistle, the red crush bars, the grey terraces, and white steps all starkly naked as the memory of the chants and the echo of footsteps is borne away on the wind. Paradoxically, the stadium is not empty. At the other end, in two of those well-fenced pens, stand the visiting fans, a posse of support that came from Birmingham to see their heroes tilt at windmills. They are told by the public address announcer to remain where they are until a police escort is readied for them so that they can be guided back to the railroad station for the trip home. Here they are, 17 minutes after it is all over, frozen in the same spots they have occupied all night, singing their songs, cheering for a side that is now bathed and dressed and talking to reporters downstairs, fans surrounded by police when only the occasional small child or newspaperman remains in the whole of the stadium. The police still watch them, watch those around them, but when the WBA fans finally depart they exit singing into an empty scene.

Down below, Joe Jordan is leaning against the wall, talking with a friend, now joined by Lou Macari, two United stars from Scotland. Again you are struck by the picture, this quiet hallway directly beneath the main stand and these men whose performances on the field excite such feelings that the visiting fans must be safely escorted out of town. Maybe there is a mystique to the uniform after all: soccer players in street clothes look delicate and young. Old Trafford is anything but delicate, though. She has the image of the steelworker, powerful and vibrant. Manchester United, unlike its sedate, urbane city center, plays to that image, throwing it forward, piling attack upon attack, but not in the stylized manner, more in the assault technique of the cavalry.

There is nothing like a midweek in England to remind a soccer fan how much the old country has influenced the game. You return to another site and see ten thousand people in a miniature version of the huge crowds and grounds; you picture the countless afternoons in the United States when games attracting only two hundred people attempt to emulate the "old country" outing. The problem with the imitation is that it ultimately proves fatal. You would do better to develop your own style and your own way.

Is English soccer a model for the rest of the world? Certainly, it has been, but its fans are not to be found elsewhere, this huge, passionate following for a game that is as English as cricket and very much more gripping to much of the population.

The game seen elsewhere, whether in New Jersey or Cologne, Brussels or Paris always falls just short of the spirit of Anfield, Old Trafford, or Wembley. The game's birthplace has the right to maintain its hegemony, even years of English failure at the highest level failing to reduce the potent power of history. Whatever the world does to the game, it is in the English fan that the love resides. Not driven by religious motivation or national pride, he is supporting his "town" team even when "town" has become metropolitan and the team representative of a country instead of a district. Traditionally the workingman's game, the spirit of commitment to hard work is appreciated here and the response of the English professional is to chase every ball, develop every line of attack.

There is not the Gallic flair or German planning to English soccer, but there is a kind of spirit and activity that seems to satisfy the "fish and chips" fan, who came to see total effort, not pretty pictures. Arsenal and Highbury may be more sedate, Wembley more traditional, but Anfield Road and Old Trafford need make no excuses. There is a heartbeat that is distinctive and a devotion that is worn on the sleeve. What American soccer team will ever have the history and power to evoke such from its fans? Perhaps the smart North Americans won't even try. For them, the idea is to entertain; for the likes of Liverpool and Manchester United, results count more, but so does a tradition that says the results must be achieved at the highest level.

Such pressure only adds to the sense of awe that accompanies a visit to the grounds.

7.

Big Match America

The American soccer scene has at least two faces: the private, nearly personal game that lives in open pitches filled with unnamed players and the gaudy, public afternoon with the professionals. The private, personal game is far older, the rock bed upon which the early success of the pros was based. The public game is slowly making a place for itself across the country just now. There is a disparity between the two faces: the purity of the initial scene versus the verve and theater of the public game; the voices of the amateur organizers who keep the weekend game alive versus the clang of the entrepreneurs who gaze at all of the young players and project a golden day of clicking turnstiles. The images overlap, the players and games sometimes equally memorable, but the private game is being eclipsed by the public spectacle with an inevitable sense of loss accompanying the elation of an emerging new day.

The small game is a weekend in the open fields, a shrill wind raking the early November twilight, a conscientious referee, having been assailed for 90 minutes by fans fueled with patriotism and alcohol, eschewing the opportunity to blow the final whistle and honorably adding five to six minutes of stoppage time. The game means nothing in any larger context, a match in an amateur league made up of players who will be back at work on Monday morning. The result of their labors is as impermanent as the weather that greeted their waking, yet there is the sense of correctness about their game that makes that referee play out the full time when it would be easier to call it finished. There is a sense of the life of the game that drives players forward into one last attack, one last tackle even though conditions and body argue eloquently against effort. Watching are a gaggle of spectators, many relatives whose attendance is social.

These are the Sunday afternoon leagues, comprising "ethnic" teams, their personnel consisting largely of recent immigrants, the baker's sons, the tailor's boy, local workers at the machine shop, high school students who came from the cities where they had only American football teams to try out for. While the players have an instinctive understanding of the game, born of their old country experiences, practice and refinement of the skills, both individual and team, is often lacking. Add in the fact that the games are often played on surfaces not suited to skill and even the rosy glow of memory does little to enhance their quality. Still, there are lessons to be learned from watching these men who can trap and control balls that the American school kid only flailed at, men who head the ball with power and direction, who run for 90 minutes without a rest.

The best Sunday games are those involving the chase for the National Amateur Cup, one of the major trophies the United States Soccer Federation offers its member teams. These could sometimes involve visitors from out of the region, Pennsylvanians from the steel towns, the legendary men from St. Louis. Yet our own players remain largely invisible, many simply known by their first names or, as often, by a nickname denoting their national origin. Hence a legion of "Scotty's" and "Stash's" and "Sal's" pass across the Sunday pitch, all looking very much alike, all part of a drama with its own impenetrable rules and regulations.

The same can be said of the onlookers, foreign-born Americans whose Sunday afternoons are occasions for recapturing days of youth, when the foreign language (English) is cast off and the bright memories of days in Palermo or Athens, Budapest or Trier or Cracow recalled in the mind as players of lesser skill and far different interests paraded in front of them. Whole families often came in the 50s, the Polish women and children dressed in the carefully tatted garments of the tourist posters, the men in their going-to-church suits, often grey and somber, their faces lined, lean hands hard from labor. We were surrounded by Polish and Italian immigrants where I watched, people brought together each weekend by the ritual of this game, men and women often saying the same thing, walking the same path around the pitch. A particularly egregious mistake by a referee would bring reams of "advice," a well-timed tackle or shot was more apt to bring a knowing smile or nod of the head than a vocal reward to the player.

Obvious to the outsider was the fact that these afternoons had two levels, the game itself carrying the pride of the players, the event of far greater significance. On one particularly cold November day, long after the professionals had made their impact in North America and the soccer world of Sunday was now peopled by tiny crowds, few families and almost no young people, a Polish friend turned his face into the strong wind and smiled as a player made a good run down the wing and crossed for a header that was just wide of goal. "I still enjoy these games," he began, "because they remind me of home. After the war there was a priest who used to give us money on Saturday mornings so that we could go to the games that afternoon. We always stood right about here, close to the field, right near the corner flag, all of us little fellows together." He could look at a scene in North America and transform it, make the players and himself wear different outfits, lift the level of play by a trick of imagination and then go home to a life that was apparently markedly different from the European one he had left behind. He probably was home in time to watch the second National Football League telecast of that Sunday and joined his children in passion for the Giants, Jets or Patriots, the region's three American football teams.

For the players there are mixed motives, from the tiniest of mercenary impulses (expense money for turning out) to dreams of discovery by some college or professional scout to just plain friendship with long-known teammates. Many who play are maintaining a regimen that has been theirs for more than half a lifetime, this business of making certain that the uniform is washed, the boots clean, the tape and liniment in the car on Saturday night. On Sunday they will form a team, play the game, then perhaps share a quick meal and conversation before returning to their other lives. Soccer is a weekend fantasy.

Transfer the game from the Sunday pitch to the weekday afternoon and only the category and the level of play needs revision: the late afternoons of the high schoolers, the Saturday mornings of the collegians, the twilight springs and summers of the boys and girls who perform in countless junior leagues. Their games, too, live in tiny capsules, vessels containing coaches, players, knot of onlookers, the importance perhaps granted by existence of some championship to be won, but the relative value of their efforts clearly delineated in the appellation "minor sport." The characteristics of these days are woven not from the same fabric of the weekend, whose ethnic origin makes soccer an important cultural experience: The American scholastic and collegiate image is a compilation of our traditional sporting values and behaviors set within the peculiar nature of this game. Cheerleaders exemplify the strange amalgam.

Unlike other games, when bounding ladies and gentlemen in fuzzy sweaters and toothpaste smiles have ample opportunity to fill in pauses with noise or to acclaim a scoring achievement, soccer's continuous movement and apparent disregard for the comments of observers renders organized appreciation unusually peripheral. As the game sweeps back and forth in front of them, cheerleaders call for "spirit" and "fight" or proclaim, "we're number one," to participants who have neither the opportunity, nor inclination, to hear their imprecations. The accumulated impact of this behavior is to render the scholastic scene significantly different from the sport across the world. The game may go on, its patterns looking like those of many another place, but the sounds are American, staccato, often unrelated to the mood of the match, sometimes apparently self-entertainment for cheerleaders and spectators who make an epic of their own presence.

The lonely picture of team manager and designated replacements accompanied by track-suited trainer making their quiet walk to the little bench tucked among spectators on a foreign ground is replaced in American school soccer by a horde, mindful of the platoons that sweep through the tunnels at the moment before kickoff in a big U.S. football game. Substitutes also comprise part of the American tableau, benches with their uniformed masses composing a cheering section of mates for the laborers on the field. The high school or college team may outfit as many as twenty-five or thirty players for a match, thus creating its own following, its own atmosphere, one that begins with collective huddling and yelling, a jumping appeal to the gods of "spirit" and progresses through an afternoon of shifting mood. Substitutes are not unaffected fans: They are assembled implorers, like hired mourners who attempt to outperform each other, players whose destiny is deeply affected by the outcome of the match. In order for their nonplaying role to have meaning, their team must be successful, lending the reserves an aura of membership in an elite body, supporting the otherwise apparently strange behavior of regularly practicing for a sport they rarely play.

The other onlookers are characteristically American as well, mirroring the campus and personality of the school they support. At the city field, the tiny crowd will be composed of knowledgeable fans, often foreign-born, who may criticize the two-referee system, the overuse of substitutes, the lack of swift skills displayed by the players, the misunderstanding of the game's strategy by coaches trained at schools from other games. They will nod knowingly at the good things, shake their heads in disgust at the mundane, and sometimes disappear before the match is done. Often you suspect they came merely to determine whether these Americans had yet managed to comprehend "their" game, had begun to shape it into a new image. It is likely that they don't quite know how to feel when departing, happy in the knowledge that a nephew arriving on the next flight from the home country will have no difficulty achieving starting status on the local side or sad that the game they love is still continually misplayed by the converts who speak of its numerous comparisons to basketball and ice hockey as if they were true.

In the suburban setting, the private game is family, but the family is the extended organization of closing decade's twentieth-century America: father, mother, sister, brother, dog, girlfriend, school friend, teacher, custodian. Father arrives late from work, the game having begun at about 3:30, the second half just underway as he strides in, jacket slung over a shoulder, briefcase locked in the car, this hour of watching the son or daughter's high school game an interval between work, dinner, and after dinner work, characteristics of the rising professional man. He joins the family that has arrived on time: Mother perhaps having no afternoon obligations to make her late for kickoff, sister and brother wandering in from their own school days to pay only token interest to the match but to revel in their identification with the town's "big school" and to begin the process of becoming part of the high school experience that will dominate their late adolescence. Their spectating will be unaffectedly personal. They will watch the number of times their player gets the ball, smile when he does something well, shriek in horror when he is placed in a position of failure. The family's understanding of the attitudes and tactics of the game is minimal and they may learn little from the weeks, years of watching. They did not come to watch the game, but to watch a son, daughter, brother, boyfriend, girlfriend. This is a point to which the entrepreneurs, with their dollar-counting blinks, have failed to attach proper significance.

Completing the scene are the few students and staff, the ones who find school life compelling enough so that their personal relationship to the institution extends well beyond its mere demands. They are truly interested in the players, in the growth and development of the young men and women they see playing. Whether they are concerned about the game is another question. They surely are interested in successful results, because they reflect favorably on the school, but they will be easily transported from soccer on Friday afternoon to football on Saturday to volleyball next Monday. Theirs is an involvement in the school and its people, not the game.

At a college campus, the picture may alter slightly. If the game has managed to achieve success, there will be an inevitable growth of support from students who enjoy the vicarious happiness that a winning combination brings. The soccer game may become an event, a date, an excuse to eat and drink beer from the omnipresent kegs, all set within a context of four largely carefree years. There is also the smaller institution, an ivy-covered scene, with former students now in their tailored tweeds, hair graying, Martini or Bloody Mary safely in hand, seated with blanket carefully spread upon the ground, picnic basket, not basket at all but a well-tuned harpsichord of material extravagance, now pausing to sip and watch the morning game they view serving as prelude to small college football that will follow. It is paradoxical to attend an American school or college match with some degree of skill and technique and be assailed by cries from such crowds urging "hit 'em again" in the best football tradition. It is also reminder of how these spectators find amazement in the game's basic skills, their "oohs" and "aahs" a reflection of the fact that they never watch the pros play on television, probably never cross the street to see anybody but the local school compete, either.

What excites an American crowd at these games, where the gatherings are intimate? Goals, certainly, to the extent that the greatest threat to the sport in the United States is the worry that somebody will tinker with the machine of the game to the extent it ceases to be soccer and becomes something else entirely. Yet the absence of goals at the average game is a problem, not because the game is any less beautiful in America, but because the game has little relative importance in any context outside itself. You understand that a European game can end 1–0 and be intensely exciting, not entirely because of the level of play, but because the game will have had meaning in a league race, a Cup competition or, quite often, in terms of somebody else's chances. The normal American soccer game exists within the most restricted of spaces, its 90 minutes important only to themselves in most cases. Perhaps you have to be in America to fully understand that even a high level of skill does not substitute for the fact that the game is often wearying when it produces few scores and average play. The emotional impact of the U.S. game is limited by its very unimportance.

American crowds are beginning to recognize some of the subtleties of the game, but they cannot be expected to divorce themselves from a background of other sports that preach constant hustle, aggression, and attack; so soccer, with its fluctuations, often seems to fall somewhere in between what a U.S. crowd has come to regard as normal. The player who does not pursue a ball that is clearly not reachable can still be target for criticism because he failed to do so. The player who gives ground to cut off space instead of immediately tackling may also be criticized by fans who appreciate physical contact more than they enjoy the games of mental chess involving use of space. The soccer team that builds slowly may find itself the target of onlookers who equate speed and motion with success. After all, the fan may have raced from one commitment to see the match and may be set to do the same again at game's end. He may find the measured approach to the game somewhat disconcerting.

They are soccer fans of a type, linked with the sport through their interest in the people who play it. In that sense, they are very like the European who may have come to follow the sport because of local links with the club or player. But in the United States, the game for friends and family isn't professional, isn't even big-time college. It is small, private, intimate and will likely remain that way. The pros of the big leagues are trying to sell a product, but these players and fans aren't necessarily ever going to be regular buyers. Instead, they are participants.

But there are the players, too, the American kids who have taken up the sport in the past decade. They are the focus of all this diverse interest and they are gradually beginning to shove aside the ethnic athletes as the base of the sport in the United States. There are several reasons why the 1980s American kid is as likely to be playing soccer as baseball or football, many of them well chronicled. An obvious answer is that the pros have sparked a desire to emulate, but that serves for a still small number of cities and does not explain why the pro game staggers in places like New England or California, where amateur soccer had long been established. A second factor is soccer's relatively inexpensive nature, an attractive feature in inflationary days, but that serves more for schools and youth organizations than it does for the individual family, which will still find the cost of a top-grade ball and shoes rather noticeable. Of importance, too, though much harder to assess, is the reaction in the United States to the Vietnam war, a time when sport was among the institutions most vigorously reassessed. Through an accident in scheduling, soccer had come to be placed parallel to football in the collegiate scholastic calendar (it could as easily have been a spring sport, challenging baseball as it does among the pros), so was available as an alternative when the gridiron sport suffered comparison with "war games" and found itself heavily attacked in some circles. It is impossible to know how much those attacks, the focus on the injury factor, and the publicity of brute force in the game, had to do with promoting soccer's popularity, but it certainly had some effect on parents. A reporter couldn't help but hear how often mothers and fathers commented on the lesser contact in soccer and the lack of apparent psychological warfare in the game. While some of the attitudes were doubtless unfair to football, which found itself whipping boy for more than a bit of the nation's frustrations with that faraway war, the result was noticeable in communities almost immediately. Boys league football began to lose some numbers to now-burgeoning soccer programs; boys league baseball, too, found that some kids preferred kicking a ball all summer.

Those factors must be paired with a fourth, however—this one the undoubted appeal to girls and women. It was 1972 when Title IX of the U.S. Education Act became law, providing equal access to education for women, who had previously been denied parity, especially in sports; 1975 when its first real impact was felt in many public school systems across the land. A goodly number of girls rushed from being cheerleaders and started to become players. One of the games they chose was soccer, presumably because it was relatively new and just starting to grow in popularity, perhaps even for the unconscious reason that in this game they could truly start at the same level as most of the boys. Today, girls' soccer is expanding so quickly that the United States Soccer Federation was able to stage its first national championship a mere ten years after the virtual birth of the game and some Northern school people are worrying that soccer will drive field hockey right out of the athletic programs.

The sport was being introduced to an entire generation of players, boys and girls who needed instruction from the most basic to the complicated levels. The demand for coaches quickly outstripped supply, the number of referees could not keep up with the games people wanted to play and the hoary institutions that make up the nation's media didn't quite know what to do about a "foreign" game that was suddenly being played by all the local kids and shouldering some of the more traditional sports off their pages. In lots of places the explosion has just begun.

Soccer's remarkable change in numbers and proficiency is most noticeable not at the professional level in America, where the imports are still markedly ahead of the native talent, but at the scholastic level. Having experienced the game for twenty-five years in Connecticut, where the sport is firmly established, having a long history before Pelé and the NASL made it avant-garde, the 60s and 70s were still eras of noticeable growth.

It began when it was obvious that soccer was attracting some of the better athletes in a school, even those schools where other fall sporting opportunities existed. There was not particularly good soccer in the early 60s, but it was clear which kids had received even perfunctory instructions from about age ten and had the rudimentary skills under control. When you reached state tournament time, these teams with better players met the ones just beginning the sport and the gap in skills was sometimes awesome. What was happening at that point is often forgotten in the rush of soccer popularity in the U.S. Given the fact that there was little organized youth soccer, the schools were doing much of the work of teaching the game. In today's environment, when it has become fashionable (and undoubtedly correct in some cases) to point out that America lacks *really* knowledgeable native-born coaches, it is fairly simple to forget that without the sport in limited areas of the country, there would have been little place to sow those seeds of the middle 70s, which fell on sparsely watered but nevertheless living ground.

A cursory glance at the 1960s records of the National Collegiate Athletic Association tournament or the logs of the USSF will show you that the sport was then completely dominated by St. Louis, the one point in the U.S. where a richly varied youth program had deep roots and was producing a volume of players. Whether it was an amateur team from Missouri, a semi-pro squad from the same state or a college team from the Gateway City or neighboring Illinois, most of the honors were reaped by the players who had the most obvious head start. As the gap has closed in the succeeding decades, the most noticeable change in the physiognomy of the game in America has been that no longer do you win soccer prizes at the youth-to-college level by merely showing up with St. Louis training. It still helps, but is no guarantee of a first class seat.

The 70s saw a great change in scholastic soccer, first an amazing leap forward, then the more gradual reassessment of possibilities and the inevitably more difficult challenges of making the framework of the game keep pace with the sudden availability of talented players. As a reporter, I was struck by what happened because the cycle was so often repeated from one community and school to another: You noticed first that the best players on a team were rarely seniors any more, each season seeming to produce more juniors, then sophomores, then freshmen who could step in and earn starting places. Then you did a tiny bit of research and discovered that a junior soccer program had started in the area, that kids were playing in spring leagues from about age ten, thus coming into high school with the basic skills already mastered. What used to be a training ground for skills, the high school team now had more good players than a coach knew what to do with. It took time, in some places, before practices were changed in nature and the emphasis shifted from how to why.

It was clear, as well, that the honors in the early 70s were going to those schools and communities where the coaches were devoting full time to soccer, not forced to divide their attentions among several sports. It meant a distinct advantage in fact to places where the mentor didn't have to move into a winter sport, then a spring sport, but could step into the community come the bright, spring weather and guide the same players in the junior program. Here, too, was where the developing role of the immigrant was most noticeable and vital, the German, Italian, Pole or Scot finally having his dream come true as neighborhood kids kicked black-and-white spotted balls. Because America won't remember in the long run, somebody ought to recognize those volunteers now: in large part, the Polish machinist who spent a day at the lathe, then coached the kids at night; the Hungarian refugee who drove all over the region to referee games for virtually no compensation; the Swede who helped everybody get soccer balls and uniforms at good rates; the college and high school coaches who voluntarily worked with every kid in town, knowing that many of them would never be "his" player. These are the unknown people in the growth of soccer. They are often frustrated ones, too, unable in some cases to understand the complicated rules that govern American scholastic sport, sometimes not able to accept the fact that the absence of soccer tradition in the States means that development of real players with a sense of the game will take far longer than the acquisition of basic skills.

Indeed, it was apparent that while the skills were bursting into bloom, the notion of team and tactics lagged far behind the vastly more competent players. This is a persistent complaint of some pros too, that American players come with the tools, but lack vision and understanding of what it is all about. It is unfortunate that our NASL professionals, themselves, don't play to the international rules, unavoidable that the pro game is an amalgam of styles forced on teams by their United Nations-type collections of athletes. While the U.S. scholastic player would undoubtedly benefit from the existence of an American style and a national coaching scheme, it seems that the emergence of both will be long in coming. Yet, this is what we are already beginning to see in the more advanced scholastic programs. Here are teams that can vary the pace of play, can score impressive victories against touring youth sides and at the highest international level. Here are players with the necessary confidence in their skills to protect the ball for longer periods of time, even when close to their own goal. Here are more naturally gifted athletes casting their lot with soccer as they see increasing opportunity for the college scholarship or professional career. Like it or not, the latter items are perhaps most important to the continuing growth of the American sport.

Another factor is that the women are apt to know just as much about soccer as the men. Not having considered sport to be a female bastion, the American male finds himself at a considerable disadvantage when it comes to this new game, not having an available store of facts, figures, and lore to toss about. Soccer does have statistics but they mean little and it does have terminology, but hardly the x's and o's that the blackboard-oriented American fan likes so much. It has its great players and super teams, but many of them turn out to be difficult to pronounce and even harder to keep straight. The game itself is so fluid that there simply is not very much time to discuss the last play since the next one has already begun.

Consider the poor volunteer coach whose kid begs him/her to donate some hours a week to the local soccer team. There are enough books on the shelves these days designed to enable the neophyte American to get through the experience, but book knowledge hardly serves to head a ball if you've never headed one yourself. Fortunately, some soccer people in the Old World don't feel that is any real hindrance. Indeed, they emphasize the need for the youngest players to merely get the chance to play, that the tactics can come later. When I spoke with Dundee United manager Jim McLean about teaching tactics, I was surprised to hear him say, "It's only at the first team level and the reserve team that you work on tactics. A team has to be together before you try to lay down a basis of things to do. Ideally, you want the reserves to do the same sort of things, but it's never the same. There is more chopping and changing with them and there isn't a Hegarty (Paul Hegarty, Scotland International centerback) with the reserves, either. You try to have them play exactly the same way but it never happens. You have to lay down a basis as the manager who says we do it this way, but there has to be the freedom for the players to take the quick throw-in or the short corner if the opportunity is there. The biggest advantage is to have the same players most of the time. Now when we make a change in the side it is usually to improve the team."

McLean is absolutely direct in his notion that young kids' teams should not be places for teaching tactics: "We work with youngsters on the skills of passing, controlling, dribbling, only on the skills. We do a lot of teaching in the one-on-one situation, the greatest sight in the game, when a player takes on and beats a defender to create a fluid situation. Let's get back to control, running, passing, dribbling, with the kids. Tactics shouldn't be taught. Then, instead of the player taking on and beating someone, you too often get a coach saying, 'Hold the ball,' or another saying, 'Lay off the man,' and you get a static situation. The playing the game emphasis is wrong for youngsters. Skills are right."

Skills have been emphasized in some of the changes in practice techniques and instruction at the American schoolboy level in the 70s. It used to be that lots of things happened in a group, but the improving abilities of the players has led to much more individual work, the "everybody with a ball" style that has proved so popular in teaching. Unlike Scotland, however, where a manager like McLean can look at relatively young players and see ten years down the road, many U.S. kids I watch regularly are still in the awkward stage of acquisition, which means that they learn quickly, reach a plateau, then don't seem to get much better. That is partly a result of too many players starting too late, but that may never be very different in America. We do have a plethora of sporting options and most kids will try more than one of them.

Of course, expanding junior competition will influence the direction of the game most sharply. While it must be doubtful that we will ever have anything like the 125 boys' soccer teams who play on a Sunday morning in Dundee, a city of comparable size at home will have enough teams to make an impact, providing the starting point for future collegiate or professional athletes. The next generation of such leagues will be different, managed as it will be by former players, largely American-born and trained. They will know something about the game, will have specific ideas about how to organize and direct young players. That, frankly, is what the rest of the world can wait a little bit longer for. As I've heard so often, "What with the way you Americans organize things to produce athletes, it's just a matter of time before you dominate soccer."

That could turn out to be prophecy if we learn our lessons well and blend the teaching with our own style of training and motivation.

8.

The NASL Game

Inevitably you go to the big cities for success in professional sports, but the impression a city makes on soccer in North America is different from its European impact. Where the Old World's stadia are usually tucked amidst row housing, hard by an industrial area, leftovers from the 20s or 30s, the American stadium is post-50s, a tribute to urban redevelopment and the hunger for large-scale entertainments, adaptable for everything from baseball to Pink Floyd.

Giants Stadium sits like an invader, a saucer that landed in the otherwise barren meadows of New Jersey. From its ramps you can see stunning Manhattan on a clear afternoon, but it is peripheral to the scenes that line the approach to America's soccer headquarters. Sweeping down the Eisenhower-era *autobahns* that re-created the United States, one sees the rolling hills of Connecticut give way to ever-increasing urban sprawl of Greater New York and New Jersey, the automobile seeming to reproduce itself on the approach to the George Washington Bridge, to spawn eight lanes of Americans headed somewhere beyond Fort Lee. Some will follow the tiny signs that say "Sports Complex," choosing the sleek four-laned efficiency of Interstate 80 or the business-laden Route 17 for their final approach to the afternoon's match, an experience decidedly non-Old-World.

When they introduce the starting lineups at Giants Stadium, the huge scoreboard flashes a picture of the player on the screen as he trots onto the playing field. When there is even a hint of excitement, the same screen shows the audience a television replay of the action and the scoring of a goal is greeted by animated revelry, a burst of official team music and the excited cries of the public address announcer confirming the name of the scorer. It is United States pro soccer, a blend of game and entertainment techniques that contrive to sell the sport to a new public.

"It's part of the American way of life to treat a sporting event like a picnic," says Tulsa coach Charlie Mitchell, a Scotsman who now earns his living in the New World of professional soccer. "When you can come into the game with your family, that's the future of sport. It should be a day out. The soccer feels like home, but outside the scene in Tulsa is very Western, cowboy boots, ten-gallon hats and all that. But we have twenty-five thousand kids playing in Tulsa and we're the only professional sport in Oklahoma so the players (his Roughnecks) are the big boys around town. I think some of the players may miss the environment of home, for the topic of the average worker is not the game as it is over there, but that will come with time."

Giants Stadium represents the apex of the professional experiment in the United States, the spot in the Meadowlands of New Jersey where it all took root in the summer of 1977 and turned a struggling franchise into one of the world's rich, name teams. Tulsa is another side of the American success story, an unlikely place to expect a foreign sport to take hold, a place with little soccer heritage and less historic connection with the game's star players and teams. In New Jersey the crowd is a combination of family groups and "ethnic" fans, the team a blend of world-class stars and big names, big salaries and plenty of pressure to produce. In Tulsa, the crowd is American; there is no pressure to import players of particular national background and Mitchell says the key to acceptance is that the fans "appreciate hard work and effort." That's certainly in line with traditional American values.

There are other voices too:

"At home we really care about the game, about who wins. If the referee makes a bad decision that costs a team a match, he'll be lucky to get out of the stadium. If the coach makes a bad substitution that costs the team a game, there will be two pages of the newspaper asking why and analyzing what he should have done. Here, they are only interested in selling hot dogs and beer." So speaks a recent arrival in the United States, a man who regularly attended North American League matches in New York and Foxboro, but one who failed to find exactly what he was looking for in terms of commitment, intensity or interest. "I know the names of the great players," he says, "but here I only bother with the numbers. There are no players you have to know by name except the great ones we already knew."

The North American League must cater to all elements of fans, the suburban Americans who might cheer as loudly for an offside goal as for a real score, unaware that the first one doesn't count until the public address man tells them so, and the well-educated soccer devotee from Europe, the Orient, the Middle East, or Latin America, fans who appreciate the history and nuances of the game and criticize those who play without apparent knowledge of such important facts. To achieve a balance, the American professional team has had to walk a narrow, difficult path between a marketing-promotional show and pure soccer—with the result that the American game is criticized in foreign circles for having too much of the former and criticized at home for lacking enough of the latter.

More dramatic than the play however, is the manner in which the game is presented here, with every contest including the trappings that might only be associated with the most important Cup final on the Old Continent. That Giants Stadium scoreboard is only part of the sideshow in New Jersey, the total scene quite different from anything in Europe. As you approach the Meadowlands on game day there is the initial sight of acres of paved parking space, already inhabited some two hours before kickoff by families who have brought their charcoal cookers and are settling down to prepare a pregame meal of nearly formal proportions, while the children are busily engaged in playing soccer in the empty spaces of the big lot. The colors are gaudy, a collection of Cosmos shirts, shorts, hats, pennants, flags, soccer balls, drinking mugs, decorated cars, signs, painted bed sheets. The atmosphere is enhanced by strolling Dixieland bands entertaining these early comers.

Striking about the gathering is its composition, very unlike the average soccer crowd in Europe, which is composed almost exclusively of very young males and the devoted adults. Here the fans are families, teenage groups out on dates or outings, college kids in groups of twos and threes. Noticeable, too, are the foreign-born fans, the ones who maintain something of the Old-World tradition by arriving just before kickoff and staying largely within the groupings created by their Italian-American, Polish-American, or German-American clubs. Yet even they are likely to have slapped a Cosmos bumper sticker on the auto or have one of those tiny soccer balls with a New York logo hanging from the rearview mirror. Grudgingly, they adopt a part of the American scene.

Inside, there is enough happening so that some detractors would say that soccer is secondary. There are bands, dancing girls, Bugs Bunny cavorting with a huge soccer ball and an equally large carrot, outfitted ball persons (not ball boys or ball girls, but Cosmos Ball Persons), continual chatter on the public address system, which identifies the player in possession throughout most of the game. The announcer also promotes various Cosmos attractions, sells tickets, or thanks somebody for providing automobiles for the players, their preseason hotel, or something else that has been worked out to both sides' benefit, while the computer-controlled scoreboard keeps the under-ten audience rapt when the game won't. Is all this necessary just to get people to come to a game of soccer? Not in Europe, perhaps, but it appears that it is an essential part of the package in the States. When some clubs cut back on their promotional items they discovered that some of the fans stayed away: not everybody, it seems, was there just for the soccer.

In Europe, the start of a match will be greeted with roars, horns, whistles, banners, flags, and song. This initial burst soon gives way to concentrated watching and the occasional vocal reward when a play is worth acclaim. The American crowd is more distracted, less educated in the sport, more apt to respond with an "ooh" at a clever play, disbelief replacing admiration that might be the pattern elsewhere. Some fans are distracted by the omnipresent sales people who meander through the stands to hawk their wares oblivious to the game around them, some distracted by the sideshows, which are never ending. It is almost as if the game itself must intrude on all of its surroundings in order to gain response.

It is partly all this which makes soccer difficult to evaluate here, leaves one uncertain whether the growing crowds prove interest in the game or suggest reams about modern entertainment marketing techniques. When a goal is scored there is the explosion of joy that greets a score anywhere, perhaps the burst of enthusiasm leading to a chant or two of "Cosmos, Cosmos," but the behavior will soon return to its normal cast and the afternoon will meander to its end, punctuated only by the fans counting off the closing seconds as their voices enliven the electronic clock with "Five, four, three, two, one."

The overseas visitor who goes to the Meadowlands will find little of himself and his childhood in these new surroundings. He will see the game as like his memory, but much else will defy integration into the preconceived notion of the soccer afternoon out. If he comes searching for the ambience of Dundee, Liverpool, or Frankfurt, he will not find it, so American has the atmosphere become. That distance from Europe to East Rutherford, New Jersey, from a place on the terraces to the corridors of Giants Stadium and an empty arena's press box three hours before the kickoff of America's biggest soccer game, is measured not only in atmosphere, but in ideas and point of view. As I sat in a now-filling stadium a voice from behind was "analyzing" the game. In rapid succession, from American voices, I heard the recommendation that the offside law be abandoned in this country, that the scoring system be changed to award more points for a goal, that maybe the goals ought to be bigger. It is this kind of opinion—and remember that is conversation between people who presumably report on soccer games—that scares the daylights out of the world. But, accepting or not, I'm about to watch a different game anyway: It is close to soccer as it is played around the globe, but fundamentally changed in these ways:

- There is a 35-yard line that replaces traditional midfield offside.
- The game will be played over 105 minutes, if necessary, not the traditional 120 when extra time is added to the 90 normal minutes.
- If scores are still level, a Shoot Out will decide the winner.
- And, oh yes, the extra time is "sudden death."

I suppose we are used to these aberrations by now, but they still seem to be just that; behaviors that alter the game by little bits and pieces. The disturbing factor is that in all of the ride down from Connecticut that

morning, in the hours of that week when the anticipation of the title game was building, not once did the
thought intrude to remind me that what I'd see isn't the
same game I had seen in Britain.

Yet it is not that Soccer Bowl is so unusual, but that it
approximates so much; not that the American professional game is a strange, somehow alien form that at-
taches itself to another body and attempts its parasitic
peace; it is the fact that so often the afternoon comes so
close to achieving the impossible, a real transfer of sport
and culture. With eyes closed, only the sound of the ball
and players to create the scene, there would be the
chance of complete immersion in the idea. But even
with eyes closed there is the intrusion of the public address, his droning mention, his stream of messages
breaking the tableau. Even with eyes closed there is the
crispness, the newness of the surroundings, a modern
world inhaled instead of an older one, the aroma of the
food and drinks carried on the winds a contrast to those
of Britain, the very crinkle of the shoes and the rustle of
the clothing—polyester against the wool of memory.
Even with concentration focused entirely on the match,
the configuration of player, lines, and ball, the universal
movements that are definition of the exercise, there is
intrusion. But the experience is close to capturing the
idea. We have come remarkably near to recreating the
scene.

There are other, intruding pictures: the well-dressed,
well-organized army of young men and women, public
relations people who turn the scene into stage-managed
production, even to the extent that somebody has an answer to every question. The marvelous magazine-thick
program, which the fan can peruse at leisure, is a mas-
terpiece of promotional literature about the game, the

league, and the day. The orchestration of events, from the pregame marching drum corps to the postgame presentations and lap of honor—all are signs of modern American sporting production. This combination of public relations, personal relations, and a sporting event, this linking together of "Have a nice day," and the concepts of competition and merchandising make up a setting that is so manifestly American.

It wasn't a classic game, but it contained some good soccer, some Cup final atmosphere, some near misses and a couple of disallowed goals. But the day is composed of images, not individuals, and the match is a signpost for tomorrow rather than a marker, which will be significant for soccer's past. If the game was slower, choppier stuff than you might have seen in Glasgow, the reasons are harder to find than you might suspect. The game lacked fluid motion, to be sure, but it wasn't static and it wasn't roughhouse, either.

Sometimes a championship game reaches heights, but as often it weighs itself down with importance and the result is contest that is nervy, patchy, somehow unsatisfying, the stakes too high and the players' emotions too fragile to allow them to overcome the first-night jitters. That has been the case in many a soccer Cup final, the situation in many a Super Bowl, World Series, or collegiate match at the summit. So it proved in New Jersey on a day when even the sky seemed undecided on its posture. Like the game, there were shafts of sunlight integrated with periods of subdued grey, the skies never weeping, but the glorious blue of a rich American fall day unable to push aside the haze of late summer. On the ride to Giants Stadium the city skyline had been bright and shiny, but like the anticipation of the match, the brightness was gradually replaced by shadow and the surviving image is of an afternoon that approached the very good, but you settled for occasional excitement instead.

It was not a pulsating or flowing match, one that swung from end to end in waves of thoughtful, attacking soccer, but a game that sprang to life for tiny moments, the rest defined by its own lack of new ideas. What Soccer Bowl had was a couple of teams prepared to work very hard for an honor they both obviously considered important, one that has come to mean something at the end of this first decade of pro soccer acceptance. You could tell from the attitude when it was over, the kind of satisfied sense of achievement that marked the Vancouver men in their dressing room. Good soccer? That is the hardest one for a returning traveler to answer, the game falling short in some sense, but rising far above one's worst fears. No, Soccer Bowl wasn't really like an evening at Liverpool or an afternoon in Glasgow, the pace of play slower and the composition of the crowd different. It could be the artificial surface that changes play so noticeably in America, or it could be the warmer, more humid conditions. The fact that most of the spectators at this Soccer Bowl, won by Vancouver over Tampa Bay, really support the Cosmos had its role to play, but you suspected that the same match in partisan Florida or Canada would have been as rocking as a game in Liverpool and you know that the players would have been lifted a bit by a hometown crowd. You were aware that the missing link in New Jersey was a commitment of the home fans and the tradition that goes with a Cup final. These will take time to build in America.

You really sense the difference once the game has ended. Unlike Britain, where the fans spew away from the ground, here there is the gentle exit, the slow diffusion of the crowds. Inside the stadium the media are gathering to dissect the performance, the atmosphere now clearly American, from the huge number of reporters to the kinds of questions that will be asked and answered. The NASL had constructed an interview area, a blue-curtained space in the bowels of the big saucer, fixed with chairs and a dais, podium, and microphone. As reporters trooped down the concrete passageway, where security staff and stadium help were already busy getting set to change things over for football the next afternoon, the leading figures in the soccer drama were brought to this central spot for their postgame duties. Here came Coach Tony Waiters, Trevor Whymark, Phil Parkes and Alan Ball, the quartet deemed the center of the Vancouver success story. Whymark, who scored both goals, was never asked a question, drifting off the podium and back to the dressing room as somebody else was brought in for the reporters' grilling. Ball and goalkeeper Parkes would receive some queries, the former mostly about his MVP award. It was Waiters and, later on, Tampa Bay manager Gordon Jago who received most of the interrogation. That's 100 percent American, too: Ask the coach is the first rule of postgame interviews. But what do you ask a soccer coach, the man who really cannot control the ebb and flow of the sport anyway? Ask him about mental attitude. At least that seemed to be the focus of this day. Was Waiters afraid Vancouver would have a letdown after beating the Cosmos? What kind of game plan did he bring? What had he expected from Tampa Bay? Was he satisfied with the performance? All questions that would have been equally at home if asked of a baseball, football, basketball, or hockey boss in the wake of a title game.

Before the players could take center stage, Tampa Bay boss Jago entered the room and the scenario was rearranged by the man in charge. The coach would be called next, allowing him to return to his locker room with his players, none of whom appeared before the large group. There was a key question to ask Jago, too, and you knew it would come immediately: Why had Rodney Marsh been substituted in his last game with the Rowdies? Why had the captain been taken off, in fact, immediately after testing Parkes with an 82d minute shot, the first real Rowdie attack in some spell?

"We had tried everything and he had given everything," Jago began. "I felt we could make a last gamble on speed, so I put on two fresh forwards with the hope of breaking them down. Some days you need a little luck and today it didn't come. Also, you have to make your luck." That question dealt with, there was little more to ask. There is usually no clear turning point in soccer, no fumble recovered, no three-point play that swings the tide. Thus Jago could only suggest that "Vancouver played very well," and admit that he had felt "that whatever offense got on top would do it." Jago would, no doubt, have much of a more analytical nature to say in the quiet of a Wednesday or Thursday, but this was snap judgment time, reaction time, and winners are usually much more quotable than losers.

After the conversations, collectively held with managers and players, there had been a bizarre three minutes when the American penchant for the big occasion, overcame itself. Into the tentlike room came Henry Kissinger, former Secretary of State, now a director of the NASL. He had been on hand to present the trophy. "I think this game today shows soccer has really arrived in the United States. When fifty thousand people come out for a game, you know it is a national sport and has caught on," he said. Kissinger, of course, is noted as a soccer buff, that picture of him exchanging shirts with some other diplomat in 1974 a lasting image of the man who was always able to capture a bit of the spotlight. Now he asked reporters if they had any questions. Perhaps we did, about the PLO, or SALT or the Nixon Administration, but we didn't think of them. So Henry Kissinger left, the symbol of an American sporting promotion, a man whose role had merely been to appear, to lend his name and stature to the match. There were no questions to ask him because he had nothing to do with the game.

Three quarters of an hour after the game ended, Giants Stadium's press box was nothing like Glasgow or Manchester. While reporters worked against early Saturday deadlines for their thick Sunday papers, the television sets blared out coverage of the Alabama-Georgia Tech football game as the American sports world whirred right on. Outside, other sets were showing the progress of Vitas Gerulaitis in the U.S. Open tennis tournament. Even as some men and women at Soccer Bowl produced their evaluations of the day, others were already planning on catching a plane to the next assignment, a professional football game the next day, that U.S. Open tennis, a college football game the next week. Indeed, in something like five hours in the Giants Stadium, I had rarely heard detailed discussion of soccer. Maybe American sports, like the American life pattern, is too transitory, happening so quickly within the context of television's world that the 2 P.M. game is already forgotten when the 4:30 offering begins. When is there time for perspective if the mind is constantly assailed with new sensations?

This is when you miss the walk downhill away from the British park, the stroll that allows you to shape the images and save those which are worthy of a place in the card file of the mind. In New York, instead, you hustle to finish the task at hand, climb aboard a bus to be taken back into that city center where nothing seems able to make an impact. The magic of the game is submerged by the whirl of the cars, the garish glow of the lights, the woman preaching beneath a huge American flag, the young men peering cautiously into the sex shop windows without wanting you to know they are looking. As thousands of travelers spill into and out of railway, bus, and subway stations, New York swallows the game.

9.

Indoor Soccer: "Human Pinball"

In dress they look like soccer players, but they greet their public escorted by a spotlight, the thumping refrain of an organ salute and the high-pitched words of a public address announcer whose task is to promote as much as inform. Sometimes, if in St. Louis for example, they arrive to the accompaniment of a steam whistle and clouds of smoke. They are sometimes flanked by bouncy cheerleaders, those omnipresent dancing girls transplanted by their collegiate birthplaces to the professional sports world, or led out by some vaguely animist mascot whose real function is comedian, entertainer for the night.

The game they play resembles soccer, too. Nobody is allowed to use the hands or arms save the goalkeeper and most of the old familiar skills are there, the necessity to trap and control a quick-moving ball, the required accuracy in shooting, the willingness to go into the tackle at close quarters, to risk one's physical safety in order to prevent a goal. But the field is markedly smaller, a carpeted bit of arena floor inside ice hockey boards and Plexiglas, which serve to contain players, ball, and action much as the sideboards of a children's table game keeps the marble in play. The rules are a mixture of soccer and ice hockey, the former contributing the format and players, the latter the timed penalties, extra-man attacks, short bursts of playing time, and the nonstop level of energy and action. Like ice hockey, too, the new game is made up of a series of actions, often the mistakes forced through the quickness and continuity of it all, but because the goal is bigger, the opportunities to score a bit more frequent, scores can mount more quickly than they do on ice.

In the simplest explanation, indoor soccer was born to give North American soccer players something to do between outdoor seasons, to maybe earn a dollar or two for clubs that sponsored teams in both leagues. What has developed, however, is a new game, laced with the components of America, tailored to arena and the family night out, where the pure entertainment value is more vital than the sanctity of a sport upon which the game is based. There are those who suggest that the indoor sport will help to speed the development of the American player because it will test him more often in competition and offer the chance to hone vital skills under the heat of contention. True or not, it already seems that some American players will become specialist indoor artists, the sheer weight of games scheduled by the two varieties (seventy-two contests would be the

1980 number for a player of both games) possibly dividing the players rather than transferring the skills and enriching the pool of talent. Yet such questions are not all that important in the context of what is happening indoors. There it is the action that entices and the spectators show little inclination to worry about such philosophical matters as "the role of the game" in terms of the older sport.

In fact, by 1980 there was an indoor team (St. Louis) whose attendance was greater than several North American outdoor squads and the prospect was that there would be more indoor soccer without direct connection to the outdoor game. When the Major Indoor Soccer League moved its opening date back to mid-November, which really meant players in training by October 1, and pushed its playoff final to the end of May, a half year of a soccer player's time was now committed to the arena game; and it was apparent that some pros would be content with that diet of the sport, taking summer off and recharging batteries for another year inside the hockey boards. The money, apparently, was sufficient for some to do it, too, especially if they remained active with their indoor clubs as clinicians, promoters, speakers, and season-ticket salesmen throughout the off-season.

Indoor soccer is booming for the simplest reason: it is exciting, quick-moving, and easy to see, a big ball in contrast to a small hockey puck, players close to spectators in contrast to the distances in the big outdoor stadia. The sights and sounds of the game are intimately delivered in arenas that are usually plush, often the center of things to do in the city of the 80s. Indeed, it is probably the arena, as much as the sport, which has helped to make indoor soccer viable in the New World and clearly hinders its transfer to other parts of the globe, where the downtown civic center has not become part of urban development. Given one of these sparkling, multipurpose American buildings, the city owners need something to fill them, and indoor soccer has come along at precisely the right moment to answer the call.

The contest can be enticing, involving the crowd from the very first moment. Considering that there are no indoor teams with pedigree, the sport virtually new the last decade, most of the public that chooses a two hours in the arena comes without prior commitment except to the home town area. Yet, once the ball is in play, there is an immediate willingness to cheer, to help the home side whenever it is in possession. The sophisticated soccer fan immediately might look for patterns in the play, begin to try and sort out the movements common to both games. The new fan simply watches the ball rattle around the arena, smacking into the sideboards with a thwack, careering off a body in motion, rebounding onto the Plexiglas with a thumping that includes the momentary shaking of the glass itself. It is obvious that the aim is to put the ball in that gaping goal at the ends of the arena, guarded by a lone netminder and topped by a fancy red light that is poised to notify all when the object of the game is attained. The contest is simple, yet skillful, a composite of planning and pure good fortune allied to willingness to work.

There is pushing and shoving, too, the contact borne of close quarters that enables the spectator to become sideline referee, even though his knowledge of the fine points may be limited. Close enough to see the expressions on the players' faces, to hear the shouts and commands of the actors, the fans become part of that dialogue, too. When one of these arenas is filled to capacity, the atmosphere can equal that of a huge outdoor amphitheater and one veteran player even suggested than an eighteen thousand house in St. Louis surpassed anything he had played before in Europe where crowds of sixty thousand were routine and the commitment to the game unlimited. Like a greenhouse, the indoor scene is force-fed, building on its own tightness and absence of space to magnify those very limits and turn them into positive conditions. Where the outdoor game might capture with its pattern and movements, many the result of instinctive recognition of available alternatives, the indoor version works through its tight confines, apparent traffic jams, and the frustrations of being squeezed. Players and ball all are seeking to find a way through a narrow alley toward an object that suddenly looks smaller than it truly is. All of that energy is governed by a clock that ticks away the 15-minute quarters with the same precision of America's other indoor games, the seconds winding down to the joy or frustration of the home crowd, defining the contest in their march.

The goals can come from anywhere and quickly. Perhaps it will be a low hard rocket to the corner after someone has run well to gain possession, then laid the pass back into the path of an attacker pursuing another angle of approach. Perhaps it will be sheer force, a free kick hit through or off the two-man wall set to try and give a goaltender some protection. Maybe it will result from the hectic action itself, the ball rebounding off goalkeeper, boards, Plexiglas, finally to be nudged into the net at third or fourth attempt by attackers who aren't moved out of the danger area. Or it may come off the back of one of those unfortunate defenders who attempts to help his keeper with a late lunge into position, but succeeds only in deflecting the leather past the unfortunate netminder.

The most dangerous indoor situation, the breakaway, occurs more often than on the big field, a paradoxical situation built because of the enticing nature of attack on the carpeted floor. It is necessary to involve every man in both attack and defense, hence there is the ever-present danger that in throwing men forward to seek goals, there will be that vulnerable space behind, to be neatly exploited by quick attackers set free by passes that appear long, but are really shorter than the average cross delivered on a Saturday afternoon in the fall. The space indoors deceives the player as well as fan, for once set free, the attacker behind the defender can rarely be caught, so quickly is he in position to unleash a shot against the now-isolated goalkeeper. Often the goals seem to come in bursts, separated by mere seconds on the time clock, the attacking team gaining confidence from a score and pushing forward immediately to apply more pressure before defenders can reorganize.

Throughout, the sounds are not those of soccer but of hockey or basketball, the collective sigh of relief when the locals clear the danger area, the dramatic "ooh" and "aah" when a shot whistles just past a waiting corner, just over the top of the cage. There is also the staccato applause that accompanies a dry moment in the entertainment, the isolated catcall to referee or favorite whipping boy among the players. The scene looks vastly different from traditional soccer, too, fans comfortably ensconced in theaterlike chairs, seemingly as intent on their popcorn and beer and pizza as on the action below, utilizing the occasion to picnic at the concession stands, to laugh and share family or friendly moments in the context of a sporting engagement. It is not unusual for them to exit in the middle of play in pursuit of food or souvenirs.

It may be that indoor soccer will someday assume the apparent importance of the outdoor game, that winning will become vital. Then the crowds will choose sides and will their teams on as they do in other games. To date, the sport seems too new for that, the results important in terms of building support for the home side, not very important in terms of world sport or national interest. Indoor soccer isn't up there with baseball as an American game and likely never will be; instead it is a particularly local event, one tied to the arena and the city and the league where the competition is found, perhaps fueled by some locally important names, area players who have won some public acceptance, if not national acclaim. Because there is this carnival air to the event, a sport where entertaining seems truly as important as winning, there is a difference to the occasion: The players may regard each game as vital, but the fans don't. They can be just as happy with an exciting loss as a win, but "exciting" is the key term in the equation.

Trying to define the indoor game is harder than it looks. "I wish they had called it 'sockey' or something like that because it isn't soccer," says one veteran reporter with a wince, while a veteran outdoor coach decried the version of the sport as full of "ridiculous goals" that happen simply through sheer luck. One player admits he doesn't know what makes a good indoor player and another talks about having to learn new skills, while coaches debate the merits of field organization, but keep coming back to wondering what kind of man makes the most successful practitioner of the game. One general manager likes the *Sports Illustrated*-coined term "human pinball," while another emphasizes the soccer aspects and talks about organizing little leagues of indoor players just as America has taken its kids' baseball approach to the outdoor game. Indeed, in less than a month, one team rented its practice space to ninety teams and expected more for a second cycle.

"I think you will see this game evolve in tactics with more basketball moves included. In hockey you can play the man and let the puck alone, but here you can't play the ball and leave your opponent by himself," said one college coach as he watched the new game. "I see the indoor game as an American sport," notes an MISL (Major Indoor Soccer League) mentor, "but the younger players have to learn to move the ball faster, to keep it simple but make it quick. Indoor players have to be trained for indoors, they have to learn to breathe indoors because it is different. You cannot wait for your second wind, but go all out all the time." A hockey veteran admits, "I don't know what soccer is all about, but I know a good play when I see one. A hockey player can really help a soccer player in this sport. For instance, on the power play most guys shoot for the net, but the guy beside the net is the most dangerous man. You have to aim for the winger coming in late to deflect the ball." And a veteran player, when asked why the New York Arrows were such a dominant force in the young league offered: "New York plays soccer and they have that great thing, the guy who always puts it in the net (Steve Zungul, a 100-goal scorer for his club in its second season). Two of them, really, because they've got (Branko) Segota, too, so they don't worry about being two or three behind because they just say, 'We'll get 'em back,' and keep right on playing."

Basketball, conditioning, ice hockey, or just good, old-fashioned soccer fundamentals . . . all items discussed regularly when the newest version of the sport is bandied about. But *why* all the talk, anyway, and is there truly a future for this variety of soccer? To much of the world, the idea of a player leaving a country like Poland, Portugal, or Spain to play *indoors* in North America must seem daft, but the amazingly rapid appeal of the sport and the everexpanding schedules could mean that indoors, not outdoors is the way that soccer will truly become a big American pastime. That surely would confirm all of Europe's worst fears about what the newcomers would do to their precious game.

"The player who is a great dribbler, who likes to take on and beat people one on one, may be great outdoors, but not here," says a veteran player whose career spanned soccer in Holland and North America. "Here you have to move the ball quickly, find the open man, and then get in position for the rebound. Dribbling the ball just slows the game down." Hence the moves that catch defenders off guard and create space outdoors simply let the defense get organized indoors. It could be that the more skillful player is not as useful, then, as the hard worker, the fellow who is willing to take chances, throw his body into the melee, and hope to create something by accident as much as design.

For defenders, surely, there are different sets of problems. "It is very difficult to channel a guy on a breakaway as you do outdoors, because here when the man comes at you one on one he just goes off the wall with the ball and then he's right around you," says one back-liner. "Instead of going with the man, as you must do outdoors, you have to attack the ball here. You really have to concentrate for short periods."

Those short playing periods are another major adjustment that a player must make indoors, since the sport has adopted ice hockey's pattern of continuous substitution. Unlike six-a-side soccer in the rest of the world, where the sport is essentially a training game, American indoor uses a sixteen-man roster and keeps all of those players involved in the game. It means that players are actually in the game for periods as short as one minute, rarely for spells longer than two. Although tiring for the moments when the men are in action, the sport does not add up to being as demanding as the outdoor game, at least not in the minds of some players who note that it is possible to compete two or three consecutive nights indoors, something not possible outdoors.

"I think this is a good game, fun to play, one that has a lot of spectator appeal," continues an American who has grown up during the time when soccer has made its impact on North America. "The outdoor game has taken hold, but it is taking longer than expected. A lot of outdoor aspects are still not appreciated by the fans, but indoors there is not as much buildup to a goal, not as much subtlety. This (indoor game) may have more success in some places than the outdoor game."

People who started the MISL surely won't argue that point. They conceived the league in the late 70s as a venture in pure American sporting capitalism, a sport that did not need a major television contract, a merger with an existing league, or tons of money to become successful. There may have been scoffers at first, but those crowds of fourteen thousand have obviously done something to awaken folks to the potential of the game. For people around the globe, the way the new sport has gone about selling itself could hold some interesting lessons, too.

Overseas, the community generates the team, but that has not been the case with soccer in the United States, hence the need to create the team, then make it seem part of the community. It's done with aggressive techniques, like advertising campaigns that get the team name in front of the public, those omnipresent clinics that serve to introduce the skills of the sport and its players to the young audiences, and through the inevitable speaking appearances by the players. And, in America, via television. It has already played a vital role in attracting fans to a game they had never heard of and television may be the way that the sport grows dramatically in the decade ahead. Unlike the outdoor version, the indoor game has been tailored for the commercial people, with the contests divided into four quarters, with three minutes (ideal time for selling products) set aside between the periods. That means that the cameras can follow the play for short periods of time, then cut off to a commercial message without missing any action. The fan at home gets a two-hour package, again ideal from a TV station's scheduling perspective, and, the promoters hope, he will be enticed to go out to the local arena and see the home team play next time it is in town. Between "away game" packages and cable television presentations, indoor soccer had already made a surprisingly strong impact on the tube, albeit without breaking onto one of the major networks. Unlike the outdoor game, which the MISL people are at pains to point out is not "their" sport, the indoor game doesn't think a national TV package as important, anyway.

What the cameras do capture is a game that swings regularly from end to end, with the obvious problems for goalkeepers and the attraction of the shot, itself, unleashed with just as much force as outdoors, but made to seem more powerful when struck inside the tiny arena. It smacks, whacks into the boards, sends the Plexiglas shuddering, impressing the onlooker as cannon surprised cavalry in some ancient battle. Side-wheeling efforts to get some part of the anatomy in contact with the leather is part of it, too, and it all seems to come across well on the screen. To keep the action nearly constant, the rules makers prohibit a clearance into the spectators, penalizing deliberate stuff with a two-minute delay of game penalty, which affords teams the chance to move the ball quickly, screen the goalkeeper, and put shots on net in the power play situation.

In terms of individual player skills, the consensus seems to emphasize physical fitness, willingness to maintain a high work rate, and the happy faculty of being able to play with nagging injuries. The indoor player is seemingly always going to be bumped and bruised, nursing some kind of leg or foot knock from a preceding game; and the ones who can put the aches to the back of the mind and come back for more punishment are mighty valuable. Work rate is essential, too, because the development of the indoor tactics has led immediately to the concept that everybody attacks when in possession and everybody defends once the ball is lost. The player who fails to retreat quickly into defense is a liability.

"You need a lot of runners, a couple of track people," says one indoor man, "then you need the passing up front to go with it." The runners, of course, are what American players have sometimes been characterized as, unsophisticated in the subtle ways, trying to make do with hustle instead of anticipation. Indoors, that kind of non-stop effort is often rewarded with the bounce of the ball and the rebound, which can create a scoring chance, those omnipresent boards keeping balls in play that would be harmlessly over touchlines or byelines on the big field.

If it seems that subtle skills aren't useful, that's a bit of a misunderstanding. The same kinds of well-struck passes, although over markedly shorter distances, still reap rewards indoors, but they must be kept extremely close to the ground, in deference to the fact that the ball in the air is so easily captured by a goalkeeper, unlikely to be dangerous. The low, hard-hit cross is a most effective weapon on the carpet, coming as it can through a forest of legs there to deflect it one way or another. Goalkeepers who dive regularly into that melee of bodies show the kind of courage and anticipation that American fans revel in, though those goalkeepers often pay an extremely high price for their interventions.

Close control and precision with the ball are definite factors in the indoor sport, one reason why so many American coaches are in favor of the expansion of playing opportunities. Players learn to react in confined space, recognize the need for accurate passing, and develop the ability to shift rapidly from defense to attack. For the North American player, having to perform these skills in a competitive environment, watched by crowds who like to see the home side win, the atmosphere is probably just about right. Considering that an additional forty games per year can be played, it brings the American athlete a kind of experience that has long been available elsewhere, even if a segment of his games are markedly different in overall structure.

It is this aspect that the purist must rationalize with the obvious pinball attractions of the game. If you set aside the fact that games are often decided as much by fate as plan, ignore the fact that the game going on down there in the arena really isn't all that much like soccer, then you can concentrate on the fact that the contest is a new game that drew on some, not all, of the soccer skills and grafted them onto a contest that has some interesting appeal. It is just as difficult, maybe even harder, to trap and control a fast-moving soccer ball inside as out, just as difficult to strike the first-time volley accurately, just as hard to anticipate where the shot is coming from on the breakaway. These are universal soccer skills, just as the poor pass, the badly judged cross, the miskicked chance, and the fumbled cross are all sins regardless of field size or rules of the game.

What stood out in the first couple of years of indoor play was that the great individual, like New York's Zungul, could dominate a game in the same manner as a Kareem Abdul Jabbar can take a basketball game in one hand and shake it. By their supreme ability to create room for themselves, men like Zungul or Fred Grgurev scored an inordinant amount of goals and won a hatful of games for their teams. It was partially a case of having clever mates to supply them with the ball in the proper places, but we saw enough of those two scoring completely on their own to become convinced that there is far more room indoors for the individual star than is allowed on the bigger field. These individuals can be publicized as "stars" in the new game, usually a good way to build interest and attendance. This does not mean that there are no team tactics, rather that the direction the sport develops may have more to do with talented individuals than it does with radically new ideas involving all six players.

If there does not appear to be a great prospect for revolutionary ideas in team tactics, that is not to state that the indoor game will always be played to a single pattern. Indeed, what struck me over the first couple of years, was that the games were not all the same, some teams more able to slow the pace and settle the ball. Here is a tactic that some sides will utilize to try to minimize their deficiencies in speed, although it may ultimately prove a negative approach to the game.

What makes the individual players so ultimately important indoors is that only the markedly talented man is going to be able to make that little bit of extra space to control the ball at close quarters, turn and get in the shot to the lower corners where indoor keepers seem most vulnerable. It is also a case of being able to strike the ball forcefully with almost no approach to the ball, while the indoor goal scorer also must be much more like basketball's pivotman, able to play effectively with his back to goal. One wonders just how many goals Gerd Mueller would score indoors were he now just nineteen and embarking on a career in this game. Even those balls that go into the corners require that the attacker have his back to the net, so there is a high degree of reward for being able to control, feint, and turn quickly when so placed. Zungul, the Yugoslavian star, certainly has that and the remarkable statistics to go with it.

But it may be too early to talk of stars, to figure out

what such feats might ultimately mean. The sport will take its time to season, to set its own definitions of achievement. For now, it is a remarkable success story, having enticed some public with its style, dash, and color. Its package seems one of the better sporting bets in an age when to take the plunge into the entertainment world is to gamble. Paradoxically, real, sustained growth could bode some problems for the outdoor game, especially if the entrepreneur discovers that the real soccer money in the U.S. might come from operating out of the arenas instead of the big stadia. The unpleasant fact the NASL had to face in mid-season 1980 was that in half of its franchise locations, the *average* crowd would have been seated comfortably in a Civic Center of fifteen thousand capacity. If such crowds as that can be consistently drawn indoors, then the urge to expand that indoor season at the expense of the traditional game would force players to make choices that might not always be based on their abilities and interests. It would be ironic, indeed, if American soccer interest turned out to be stronger for an ersatz game than the real thing, but hardly against the lessons of history. The United States has been incorrigibly independent in its sporting interests, remarkably secure in its own games and ideas. Indoor soccer could turn out to be another case, the world staring in wonder at a game they use for recreation and physical training suddenly blossoming as *the* form of association football that makes it big in America.

If so, then those swinging spotlights, steamer whistles, dancing girls, and prancing mascots will join the bizarre collection of colors, nicknames, and promotional jargon that have already combined to create the indoor mania.

The traditionalists can ring their hands and utter sighs of frustration when a shot shatters a piece of Plexiglas and rebounds into goal, but chances are that a couple of thousand youngsters won't care at all. They seem to think the whole thing is fun, the key to the whole future equation.

10.

America in the World Game

Having spent August 1976 in West Germany, before the euphoria of the 1974 World Cup triumph had worn off, where every team was trying to mirror that championship side, my first trip to an American game that fall was approached with a mixture of anticipation and dread. In previous years, the return to Connecticut school action paled against the memory of the summer in Europe. This was different, the combination of marvelous sun and ice blue sky, a gentle breeze, and a happy, informal student crowd ringing the University of Connecticut field contributing to the picture. The match was not truly a game, but a preseason scrimmage. The primary reason for attending was to see a local boy playing with the visitors.

The first 30 minutes showed American soccer for

what it can be. The players stroked the ball about the field with ease and skill, built their attacks rhythmically, tackled firmly and with noble sporting intent. The game was open, attractive, and fast-paced, the spectacle easily as good as that seen the preceding weekend in Munich between Amateurliga sides, one of which wore the colors of Bayern Munich. Now one shouldn't misinterpret: The two college sides at Storrs were not as good as Bayern Amateurs, many of whom graduated to the top rank and helped win the 1980 Bundesliga crown. But these two college teams played the *same* game for more than half an hour and that was a revealing, enticing prospect. It *could* happen on a United States playing field.

Because it was a preseason run, the two coaches were using the game to examine their personnel, so the original elevens were soon broken up and substitutes flooded the field. The early spell was broken, never to be recaptured. The match went the full 90 minutes, contained much good soccer and was interesting to the end but never really approached the opening third. The same can be said of many games, but the important thing was that this time the exceptional skills weren't demonstrated by foreign-born players on a pitch across the Atlantic. This was the product of American coaching and training, American player development methods. That 30 minutes of excellence entices still, for all too often the standard of U.S. play remains scrappy and unsatisfying to the seeker of art.

Anyone who has watched American soccer for a time can easily pinpoint some weaknesses in our game: Until recently, few of our top athletes ever tried the sport; the level of competition has always been below European average; the number of games played has been minimal; playing fields and conditions are often less than optimal; coaches, especially at the school level, may never have played the game and usually have not had much experience of it at world level. The litany seems endless, yet offers little in the way of real answers to the problems, for each item ticked above can be remedied without much change in the resulting product. Better athletes turning to the sport won't produce better soccer automatically, especially if they come from an environment that doesn't appreciate the sport's subtle nuances; raising competition levels may only produce games of greater intensity, not greater skill; playing an additional number of games doesn't help all that much unless those games are of a level above that of the normal college or high school match; better playing fields and better coaches will surely help, but not until conditions are such that spontaneous development of top players is already taking place. It seems certain as an eastern sunrise that coaches do not create great men in any sport: They merely serve to motivate the already special individuals while hoping to mold the remaining, often ordinary, players into an effective supporting cast.

Yet, the American kid doesn't grow up playing the game or surrounded by it. It is one of several sporting chances, a choice among many. Even as the high school youngster is playing out his season, he would be the rare American, indeed, if he was inundated with talk about the game. When his afternoon endeavors are over it is more likely that the locker room talk will be about professional football or baseball's World Series. There is virtually no chance of our players being immersed in the kind of soccer-always atmosphere that permeates Europe. With the advent of more soccer on television this may change, but slowly, so our developing player will continue to get his tactical knowledge almost entirely from coaching instead of from watching the pros just down the street. He won't be subjected to the daily collection of lore, criticism, and suggestion, either. That is the way of general public elsewhere, and perhaps that is why so many American soccer players resemble Europeans playing basketball.

As soccer in North America, basketball in Europe has been learned by players who have no early acquaintance with the sport, no social setting in which to play it. We have seen how veteran national teams like those from Russia and Yugoslavia have managed to put together effective teams, ones that challenge American Olympic supremacy, but even as they close the gap between themselves and the U.S. youths who compose our international quintets, there is a clear difference between their players and ours. What the Europeans present is an excellently-trained, well-taught group of players who have learned what to do without necessarily acquiring any flair or interpretation. When you assess them technically you discover that they often dribble as well as we do, shoot as well, rebound as well, even pass and play defense as well as individuals, but these area skills do not add up to a sum greater than its parts. The sum, rather, is less when compared to the teams of Americans who have played since childhood and bring native flair to the sport, see the openings and options without having to think of them, anticipate the moves of the other players before they become reality. Such is the difference, one that is instantly noticeable when an American player of reasonable quality joins a group of Europeans.

The American soccer player is often the European

basketball player. Through the improved coaching he has received in schools his skills are rapidly increasing. Youngsters here can probably juggle a soccer ball with as much proficiency as foreigners, trap and control the ball reasonably well, play with the chest, head, thighs, just as anyone else, but, as on the European hardwood court, it doesn't often come together as a complete player. "Do you think there is an innate soccer ability?" I was asked by a British journalist at one point. He was one who had been in the U.S. and was mightily impressed with the interest, unimpressed with the American players he had seen. "I saw your national team play at Aberdeen last year," he continued, "and there were no players of real quality standing out. I have a friend who says that the United States is going to turn out to be just like Russia in soccer. You know, a country that produces a million technically efficient players every year, but hasn't had a single one to remember. Oh, the Russians had (Oleg) Blokhin, all right, and (Lev) Yashin, but he's a goalkeeper, and you know what I mean anyway."

The analogy is too harsh on the Russians and unfair to us, but contained a given: that the United States would be quite as able and dedicated as the Russians when it got around to producing soccer players in large numbers. Would we, though, turn out ones adept at the skills but rarely creatively outstanding? And how, anyway, do you avoid the problem of producing carbon copy players when the coaching system has the complete responsibility for turning out accomplished performers but has no real fabric to fall back upon, no place to look for comparison except the television set?

What is most noticeable about the American player of the last few years is that he has become technically better without necessarily understanding some of the concepts of the sport. For example, many youngsters have vastly improved their ball control skills, but fail to comprehend the sport as one of possession. Thus many remain unsafe with their passes: "We'll get the ball right back," seems to be the attitude; but it is based on the common feeling that the other guys don't pass well, either, rather than on a true concept of the game. Second, American players have greatly increased their specialist conception without being ready to comprehend the multifaceted nature of the sport's "support" system. In the average Connecticut high school game of a decade ago, it was rare to see players maintaining a good positional sense; today it is relatively easy to tell who are the midfielders, wingers, central strikers and backs, but the systems collapse awfully quickly when somebody runs forward into space and the neophyte players fail to understand who is supposed to rotate into the vacated regions. This is like the European basketball player in a zone defense, who may do very well until the difficult concept of sliding and switching comes into account.

The problems are not of innate ability, but environment. There is certainly no reason why Europeans appear to be more adept at the game than Americans except for the obvious reason: They have been exposed to it much longer and in a variety of settings. It was never really taught, but absorbed.

The question remains: "What is the best way to prepare American soccer players?" Our traditional answer has been to develop its future professionals through the collegiate and scholastic ranks, but can soccer afford to wait long enough for a major college sport to emerge, remembering that it is only a decade since large scale growth began? There are still precious few college-level players able to step off campus and into a professional team.

There are aspects of the game as played in the United States that operate counterproductively, starting with the fact that American schools and colleges play different rules from the international game. Most important of these alterations involves the use of substitutes, perhaps in our rules for noble reasons, but fundamentally altering the manner of play. Worldwide, soccer is a 90-minute endurance and speed test, only grudgingly giving in to demands for very limited use of replacements. Much of American soccer is different, teams dressing as many as twenty-five uniformed players for a contest. The coach may then insert his additional players as he sees fit, the man removed from the match allowed to return at a later stage of play, in direct conflict with international rules. The intent may be to allow more people to play, but the result goes well beyond any worthy aim of the legislation.

An American can be encouraged to play "all out" for a short period of time rather than learning to pace himself for the duration and the coach is more effectively injected into the match as strategist and control figure, something common to all American games but strikingly missing in the usual soccer realm. By encouraging players to work hard for short bursts of time, the American rules effectively change the playing style of the developing athlete at a time when the task of pacing must be mastered. It is far different to run for twenty minutes in hot, humid weather, then sit for ten while legs and lungs recover, than it is to work the length and breadth of the pitch knowing that timing, energy-saving anticipation and knowledge of the game must suffice instead of the opportunity to rest.

It has always seemed to me that individual differences among nations derive from the manner in which their players adapt to the 90-minute rigors in their own climatic conditions. It is not so much that nations develop different styles of soccer, but that the techniques that work in one environment often fail in another. The North European player can surely produce a higher work rate than his Floridian or Brazilian counterpart. It is often considerably cooler at the height of a North European summer, than at Disneyworld on a February afternoon. In hot climates, one will see players opt for walking time, while the European midfielder is known for his persistent chasing, never-yielding attitude. South Americans have been know to "stroll" through matches, bursting into top gear only when the scoring opportunity presents itself. The young American, however, is likely being reminded that he can get a seat on the bench if he tires, a spot that denies him the essential need to adapt to his conditions. Instead the game has been adapted for him.

The role of the American coach must be examined in contrast with the world game, too. Clearly the rise in coaching competence and commitment, particularly in the last two decades, has helped the soccer revolution in America. These coaches, especially at scholastic level, exert a far greater influence than their counterparts around the world, American mentors still often teaching fundamental skills to youngsters who would have acquired them before formal coaching in Europe. Because the coach is so vital in the American scheme the basic question about the U.S. version of the sport must be asked: Do American soccer coaches ultimately have to have center stage or can a sport grow in our country without being coach centered?

Men who have been raised in our setting, even if their primary interest is soccer, must look at the international game and wonder just what is going on. They turn on their television set and see the English Cup final. Where are the coaches? Sitting next to one another, virtually, in the stands, well-removed from the action, watching almost like any two other spectators. They aren't down there on the sidelines to pace and exhort, haven't got a headphone on to receive instructions from the scouts high above the playing field, aren't waving play books or beckoning substitutes at every turn of fortune. Clearly a soccer game is supposed to be in the hands of the players once the kickoff occurs. Soccer coaches must be teachers, teachers whose pupils are regularly examined in public, by somebody else's methods.

American coaches can hardly be blamed for wanting to have more control than this, especially if their income is to depend on game results. At the moment that may hardly be the case at most U.S. schools but the day is coming when collegiate soccer will experience some of the same high pressures already visited on football, basketball, and other mentors. Those very pressures could lead to soccer becoming more, not less, coach oriented in America. One can foresee the fragmenting of coaching tasks, but, one hopes, nothing like the huge staffs that man U.S. football and basketball programs, where the relative stature of coaches can sometimes be assessed by enumerating the assistants who surround their leader.

The role of the coach will be worked out over the coming decade, just as the rules will no doubt gradually come into line with those of the world, but any American who knows when the synthesis will be complete has thus far remained silent. What remains is the attractive lure of a September afternoon, 30 minutes of pure gold, which showed that the American game can match its foreign rivals, if only it will be allowed to do so.

I don't genuinely expect that Americans will ever imbue soccer with the importance that it holds for a Scot or Englishman or Brazilian, but I remain optimistic that at some distant point, the sport will be allowed to exist on its own. Outgrown will be the promotional devices to try to "Americanize" the game, gone will be the "hot dogs and beer" mentality that characterizes too much at the upper level.

Perhaps the Sunday afternoons of the future will again be spent on unfenced fields, crowds surrounding a venue where unknown athletes chase dreams and meaningless results. The difference then will be that the English will be unaccented and the players drawn from an American background. The audience will not resemble a picture postcard and the nostalgia will not be for a land once home, an experience linked to a nearly forgotten past. The game played will be for itself, by Americans.

We may, someday, win a World Cup or take a major club championship. If so, it will happen because the growth of the professional sport was steady, unspectacular. The entrepreneurs who boosted the game in the middle 60s will deserve their share of the credit on that successful afternoon, but it is only a share, not the total. We have always had a soccer heritage in the United States, one markedly different from the British Isles, one separate, in fact, from the rest of the world. That is the heritage we must build on.

Jerry Trecker is a sports writer for the *Hartford Courant,* a regular contributor to *Soccer Monthly* and *Soccer Digest,* and a Connecticut high school teacher. He travels often to Europe in order to pursue his tremendous interest in soccer. His wife, Janice Law Trecker, uses these journeys to gather background material for her mystery novels.